AUTHORITY
FIGURES

AUTHORITY FIGURES

RHETORIC AND EXPERIENCE
IN *John Locke's*
POLITICAL THOUGHT

· · · · ·

Torrey Shanks

The Pennsylvania State University Press
University Park, Pennsylvania

Library of Congress Cataloging-in-Publication Data

Shanks, Torrey, author.
Authority figures : rhetoric and experience in John Locke's
political thought / Torrey Shanks.
pages   cm
Summary: "Examines the place of rhetoric in John Locke's
political and philosophical thought. Traces the close ties
between rhetoric and experience as they form the basis
for a theory and practice of judgment at the center
of his work"—Provided by publisher.
Includes bibliographical references and index.
ISBN 978-0-271-06504-5 (cloth : alk. paper)
1. Locke, John, 1632–1704—Views on political science.
2. Political science.
3. Rhetoric—Political aspects.
I. Title.

JC153.L87S53   2014
320.51'2092—dc23
2014019308

For AMBARISH *and* JASPER, *with love*

CONTENTS

In this book, I uncover the importance of rhetoric as figural and creative language for John Locke's political and philosophical critique. This project may, at first glance, seem counterintuitive. Locke, after all, presents himself as a thinker and writer who should have little use for linguistic flourish: a man of science, a plain speaker, and a humble philosophical underlaborer. We need look no further than the epistle that opens *An Essay Concerning Human Understanding* to find this modest figure in search of knowledge when "*Vague and insignificant Forms of Speech, and Abuse of Language, have so long passed for Mysteries of Science.*"[1] He expresses the hope that this book, composed of his "hasty and undigested Thoughts," marked by repetitions and his "*discontinued way of writing*" (7), might help others to "*avoid the greatest part of the Disputes and Wranglings they have with others*" (14). While the author's intentions are good, he confesses to an artlessness that would seem to prevent him from offering anything other than unadorned truth. "*I have so little Affection to be in Print, that if I were not flattered, this Essay might be of some use to others, as I think, it has been to me, I should have confined it to the view of some Friends, who gave the first Occasion to it*" (9). Would we expect anything different from the empiricist philosopher or the political theorist who returns to the first principles of natural right and law?

A certain skepticism is understandable. But if we take seriously Locke's sober commitments to natural, to say nothing of moral and political, philosophy, then we must take a closer look at his own story of how the *Essay* came to be. The "*History of this Essay*," featured in the epistle, depicts the personal situation that launched the pages that follow:

> I should tell thee that five or six Friends meeting at my Chamber, and discoursing on a Subject very remote from this, found themselves quickly at a stand, by the Difficulties that rose on every side. After we had a while puzzled

our selves, without coming any nearer a Resolution of those Doubts which perplexed us, it came into my Thoughts, that we took a wrong course; and that, before we set our selves upon Enquiries of that Nature, it was necessary to examine our own Abilities, and see, what Objects our Understandings were, or were not fitted to deal with. *This I proposed to the Company, who all readily assented; and thereupon it was agreed, that this should be our first Enquiry.* (7)

What began as a private conversation among members of the Royal Society, interrupted and redirected by a sudden eruption of uncertainty, is transformed into a collective inquiry into epistemology, psychology, and language, undertaken with the assent of each participant. This project, the epistle shows, is a civil encounter, conducted with a care for the judgment of each individual and cognizant of their limited capacities. It is not only these five or six friends whom the author engages in inquiry, however. The epistle also invites the reader into his intimate circle by appealing to the reader's own judgment: "*If thou judgest for thy self, I know thou wilt judge candidly; and then I shall not be harmed or offended, whatever be thy Censure*" (7). The invitation interpellates the reader in the same modest terms that the author has set out for himself: the Essay "*was not meant for those, that had already mastered this Subject, and made a through Acquaintance with their own Understandings; but for my own Information, and the Satisfaction of a few Friends, who acknowledged themselves not to have sufficiently considered it*" (7). This is only the first such instance in which the *Essay* gestures toward the reader as fellow inquirer and ultimately fellow judge. Locke further encourages readers to compare their experience with the claims of the *Essay*, establishing a mirroring relation between author and reader, as in this early claim about the importance of clear language: "*There are few, I believe, who have not observed in themselves or others, That what in one way of proposing was very obscure, another way of expressing it, has made very clear and intelligible*" (8).

In presenting himself and the origins of his essay as lacking in eloquence and design, Locke performs here more than the trope of modest and reluctant authorship. He reveals himself as an architect of philosophical and scientific inquiry as collective undertaking not only between fellow scholars but also between reader and writer. The civil conduct inaugurating the inquiry of the *Essay* signals Locke's social and philosophical commitments as an early English empirical scientist, under the influence of Robert Boyle and other luminaries mentioned by name in the epistle (9–10). It is this performance, in the epistle and throughout the *Essay*, that is emblematic of what Richard Kroll in *The Material Word* calls the culture of Epicurean materialism. Inspired by the ancient materialist philosophy of Epicurus, preserved through the poetry of Lucretius, early moderns reinvented Epicureanism for the needs of the new experimental science. They emphasized probable judgment based in experience over certainty and demonstration. In contrast to their ancient forerunners, they sought to reconcile materialism with Christian belief, all the while remaining cognizant of the ineradicable contingency of the human condition. And unlike their Cartesian and Spinozan contemporaries, rhetoric was understood as essential to cultivating the proper conduct in science, philosophy, and, as we will see, the human understanding itself.

In the pages that follow, I pursue this insight that Locke's seeming estrangement from rhetoric in fact signals a host of philosophical and rhetorical engagements that shape his account of judgment based in experience. His complex relationship to rhetoric, at once positive and negative, I will argue is fundamental to the critique that he launches against philosophical authorities of his day and to his project of *authorizing* his distinctive mode of judgment. Situating Locke in relationship to Epicurean materialist culture invites us to give proper attention to the interplay of style and substance in the *Essay*. In my doing so, his reliance on particular figures and styles, as well as invention, comes into focus. Creative rhetoric, or rhetoric as imaginative language, emerges as essential to the movement from experience to critique in the *Essay*.

The implications of Locke's Epicurean materialism are not limited to the philosophical concerns of the *Essay*, however. For it is in the *Two Treatises* that we see the centrality of judgment to Locke's political theory. In fact, the preface to that classic work of political theory, like the epistle to the *Essay*, signals its appeal to, and defense of, judgment. As Locke again apologizes, this time for the missing middle section of the *Two Treatises*, he conveys confidence that his interrupted discourse will still provide sufficient evidence that "*my Reader may be satisfied.*" As he appeals to his readers' judgment, Locke seeks to justify "*to the World*" the judgment of the people of England. It is they who "*saved the Nation when it was on the very brink of Slavery and Ruine*" and it is their consent that makes good King William's title (*Two Treatises*, 137). It is, in other words, the judgment of the people in establishing rule and in resistance to overreaching authority that Locke seeks to justify before the further judgment of his readers. The conduct of the author, in the *Two Treatises* as in the *Essay*, repeats the cautious gesture of apology for his writing to the reader and then embarks on what he hopes, but does not insist, will culminate in assent to shared judgments. The judgment of the English people in recent political memory and of Locke's readers together, he seeks to show, is the condition of authorizing, perhaps once and for all, or perhaps not, such new and potentially fragile political conditions.

But where is rhetoric here in his appeal to judgment for politics? In politics, as in philosophy, Locke sets himself up against noise and wrangling, that is, against pernicious political rhetoric: those *"Contradictions dressed up in a Popular Stile, and well turned Periods"* of Locke's adversary, Robert Filmer. Should readers doubt his charge, they are invited to conduct their own experiment, modeled after Locke's own project in the *First Treatise*, by stripping *"Sir Robert's Discourses of the Flourish of doubtful Expressions, and endeavor to reduce his Words to direct, positive, intelligible Propositions, and then compare them with one another"* (137). Should they choose to follow suit, they will quickly find *"there was never so much glib Nonsense put together in well sounding English"* (137–38) Locke solicits an alliance with his readers around plain speaking and the careful testing of propositions. While he rails here against rhetoric, or at least rhetoric from a particular source, he also shows a concern for words and their effects, especially in politics. As we take in his self-presentation as a plain-speaking philosopher and theorist of politics, we should pause to consider that it is Locke himself who raises the question of style as important for politics. And so this book investigates the varied and creative uses of rhetorical style and figure that he adopts to challenge and rework the persuasive force of claims to political authority. I do so not because it necessarily undermines Locke's philosophical or political commitments, but because it constitutes further expression of them. In short, we do not fully understand the critical projects of the *Essay* or the *Two Treatises* without attention to the practices of style and invention through which they are brought to life for a judging readership.

The culture of Epicurean materialism in late seventeenth-century England presents a vantage point from which to consider the essential and productive contributions of rhetoric to Locke's philosophy and political theory. To take up this vantage point does not require a denial of other intellectual influences or legacies with which Locke is sometimes affiliated: liberalism, republicanism, empiricism, to name a few. Highlighting the creative reinventions of language and arguments that make up Locke's two most significant works of philosophy and political theory offers up new and diverse ways that his ideas might come alive to readers today. As I will argue, there are productive new avenues opened up from Locke's thought through a renewed encounter with these well-known texts and their engagement with the early modern politics of rhetoric, passions, and imagination.

Because this encounter challenges the familiar rendering of Locke as forwarding the "man of reason" in philosophy and politics, it speaks in unexpected ways to late modern readers, especially, but not only, to the critical readings of Locke's thought in feminist and postcolonial thought. As we will see, exploring the essential contributions of rhetoric to Locke's philosophical and political thought requires more than a general treatment of rhetoric in relation to logic or philosophy, though that can be important. It will call for locating the constitutive and creative work of rhetoric in its particular forms, especially those figures, styles, and stories that Locke uses to subvert and transform his opponents' arguments and generate new meanings and perspectives. Considered in this way, Locke's writings offer up an unexpected but robust site from which to explore the indispensable role of rhetoric for critique that proceeds from within the particular language and practices of politics, but is not bound to their reproduction.

ACKNOWLEDGMENTS

There are a number of people and institutions that have helped this book come into existence and deserve thanks. The project advanced at key moments thanks to the support of the Rockefeller College of Public Affairs and Policy of the University at Albany, the University of British Columbia, and Northwestern University. Northwestern offered me a small and richly interdisciplinary environment that has indelibly shaped my intellectual interests, especially in the Paris Program in Critical Theory led by Samuel Weber. It was my great fortune to present my work to the political theory community at UBC, and especially to have Barbara Arneil as a colleague. At SUNY Albany, I am grateful to David Rousseau and Julie Novkov for supporting research and family leave as well as organizing a manuscript workshop. The comments that I received in this workshop were both generous and useful in bringing this project to completion. Thank you to Douglas Casson, James Farr, Don Herzog, and Melissa Schwartzberg for this.

Over the life of this project, I have enjoyed the encouragement of close friends, both fellow academics and bemused onlookers. Thanks to Jennifer O'Donnell Erbs, Geneviève Rousselière, Zakir Paul, Jessica Keating, Jenny Peterson, Lisa Fuller, Sudarat Musikawong, Stephanie Olson, and Ron Schmidt. Conversations with and welcome criticism from a number of political theorists have enriched this project: Dean Mathiowetz, James Martel, Vicki Hsueh, Jimmy Klausen, Patchen Markell, Michaele Ferguson, Davide Panagia, Mary Dietz, Kennan Ferguson, Ivan Ascher, Karen Zivi, Jill Locke, Cristina Beltrán, Asma Abbas, Andrew Dilts, Robyn Marasco, Libby Anker, Matt Scherer, Cricket Keating, Brian Danoff, Laura Janara, Bruce Baum, and Mark Warren, in addition to anonymous reviewers for *Political Theory* and Penn State University Press. Several graduate students offered valuable support as research assistants on this project: Christine Klunk Dow, Sean McKeever, and Reed Williams.

I happily find myself part of a thriving theory community in upstate New York, centered around the SUNY Albany political theory workshop. My colleagues, Morton Schoolman and Peter Breiner, have been continuously supportive and encouraging. The lively circle of feminist political theory that I share with Laurie Naranch and Lori Marso has made Albany feel like home.

I am fortunate to have had teachers, advisors, and intellectual interlocutors who remain unparalleled models for me of rigorous and creative scholarship in political theory. Although not connected with this project, Michael Rogin and Hanna Pitkin first introduced me to the study of political theory, and its relation to language and culture especially. This project benefited greatly from Kirstie McClure's generous comments, which have richly repaid close rereading and rethinking (both the comments and Locke). I am grateful to Bonnie Honig, whose seminars first introduced me to Locke's *Essay* and its strange and fascinating denizens. Her insightful comments have often inspired me to think more expansively and creatively. Thanks to Linda Zerilli, whose exemplary engagement in political and feminist theory has taught me so much. Her ongoing support of this project has been invaluable.

I am grateful to my family, who have followed the ups and downs of this project for many years and provided much needed breaks from it: my parents, Janetta and Noel Shumway and Ralph and Lisa Shanks, as well as Laurel Shanks and Mark Wegner, John Thompson, and Shailaja and Ramesh Chandra, and not least, Clover, my cosmopolitan cat. Thanks to Brandi Alund-Welsh for her outstanding care for my son.

There is no repaying the debts of patience and support from my partner, Ambarish. I can only say happily that in other futures, there will now be other projects, for both of us. I most look forward to continuing our shared project that arrived just as this manuscript approached completion, our son, Jasper Bal, who brings joy and havoc.

RHETORIC AND SITUATED POLITICAL CRITIQUE

The emergence of modern political theory in the seventeenth century marks a watershed moment in which new conceptions of human reason take center stage in theorizing the foundations and limits of political authority and community. This elevation of modern reason is widely seen as bringing about a break with the rhetorical tradition, inaugurating a supposed hostility between rhetoric and political theory that continues to resonate today. In this book, I challenge this assumed enmity between political theory and rhetoric through the unlikely figure of John Locke. Traditionally cast in a dual and decidedly modern role as rationalist in political theory and empiricist in philosophy, Locke is rarely seen as a friend to rhetoric. This opposition confirms latter-day assumptions about reason's incompatibility with rhetoric that are familiar to late modern readers. By contrast, historians of rhetoric, philosophy, and science provide compelling reasons to reconsider this opposition in the early modern period, especially with regard to early empirical philosophers such as Locke. Locke's relationship to the rhetorical tradition, as we will find, is better understood as one of debt and denial.[1] While Locke undoubtedly voiced criticisms of the power of eloquence to lead us astray, I contend that Locke draws on rhetoric in fundamental ways in both his philosophical and political writings. Specifically, his appropriation of elements of the rhetorical tradition is indispensable for his critical engagements with philosophical and political authority. Rhetoric offers Locke a productive and creative capacity that sustains his challenge to reigning doctrines of his day as well as his reimagining of social and political membership. Locke's debt to rhetoric undergirds his new vision of political community reliant upon an ongoing practice of critical judgment.

Rhetoric and Political Theory

The notion of the lasting significance of a momentous break in the early modern period between rhetoric and political theory is given particularly clear formulation by Bryan Garsten in *Saving Persuasion*. Garsten identifies a "rhetoric against rhetoric" in the work of Hobbes, Rousseau, and Kant that inaugurated a powerful legacy of suspicion and distrust of rhetoric in political theory. Juxtaposing the treatment of rhetoric and politics by Aristotle and Cicero with the work of these early modern critics, he shows how a particular modern distrust of rhetoric is inextricably tied to a suspicion of persuasion and political judgment more generally. The lasting effects of this hostility between rhetoric and political theory persist today—most notably, for Garsten, among those theorists who seek to ground democratic deliberation and authority in rational rather than persuasive discourse. By contrast, Garsten seeks to revalue political judgment that appeals to arguments and audiences located on the contingent terrain of politics, and for this he turns to the insights of the rhetorical tradition. Rhetoric, in this tradition, is not restricted to "merely" eloquent speech; rather, it involves a mode of action and interaction of situated political actors and spectators seeking influence and appealing to one another's judgment. Moreover, we find that the status of rhetoric is a central question for the practice and theory of politics. This was clearly the case for early modern theorists, and it should be recognized as such by political theorists today.

Saving Persuasion rightly invites us to see rhetoric as centrally important for political thought, but its definition of rhetoric as "speech designed to persuade" puts significant limits on this relationship.[2] To conceive of rhetoric in terms of persuasion is an important corrective to political theories that assert the need for an external point or prior agreement from which to assess social and political arrangements. Appealing to judgment from "within our existing opinions" recalls political theory to the finite terrain of politics, marked indelibly by disagreement between diverse opinions and beliefs of passionate actors.[3] Working with such a narrow definition, however, cuts short the political possibilities and projects that rhetoric might sustain. In particular, a politics of persuasion cannot account for the possibility that existing opinions and beliefs, serving as the grounds of judgment, may prove inadequate to current and emerging political conditions. A political community may find existing categories inadequate because of unpredictable events or the contingent consequences of human action, such as the novelty that characterizes both political freedom as well as the rise of totalitarianism, as Hannah Arendt reminds us.[4] A political community, or some part of it, may need to challenge common opinions and beliefs because they are inadequate to their claims of freedom or justice. A rhetoric identified only with persuasion among existing opinions cannot provide the basis for this indispensable form of critical judgment.

How do political communities generate such new categories for challenging social and political arrangements? If they come from within established norms and practices, how can they achieve critical purchase on the status quo? These questions invite many to assert that claims to freedom and justice require a position external to politics, detached from customary practices and prejudices. Such an external position can be found in Rawls's original position as well as in Habermasian arguably quasi-transcendental norms arising from, but ultimately transcending, specific historical and cultural locations. In their seeking universality, it is precisely their ultimate detachment from particular social and political contexts that is a necessary condition of their normative purchase.[5] Rhetoric and imagination may even be brought into the service of this desired detachment in the form of thought experiments and exemplary rhetorical cultures. Yet the goal of such an external standpoint toward politics, whatever its debts to rhetoric and imagination (avowed or not), posits a fundamental distrust of the political judgment of the people.[6] The idea of a view from nowhere, the Archimedean point, signals a flight from politics in general and democracy in particular. It is only through politics that relations of justice and the conditions of freedom are secured in practice, that is, as lived experience.

Extending this critique further, we must keep in mind that insofar as such an external position is linked to abstract universalism, aspiring to detachment from particular political conditions limits the normative value of the plurality and material differences that condition and constitute political life.[7] Abstract universal norms often have been credited with delegitimating practices emphasizing class-, sex-, or race-based distinctions. Through their abstract and universal character, however, the validity of such norms is achieved by virtue of a perceived break with the embodied, socioeconomic, and cultural particularities of social and political life. So generating new categories for judgment, in this vein, also requires a flight from the plural and material conditions of political life. For this reason, *situated* political critique—that is, critique for which the contingent and particular relations and practices of politics are both condition and object—poses what appears to be a dilemma: how can we gain critical purchase on our social and political arrangements if our criteria are generated from within those practices? How, in other words, can political critique be enacted from within the field of politics without reproducing the status quo?

The politics of persuasion cannot respond to this problem of situated critique. It cannot respond because judgment appealing to existing opinions alone does not account for the emergence of new ways of understanding existing social and political practices or ways of envisioning how they might be otherwise. That is not to say, however, that there are no other resources in the rhetorical tradition or early modern political thought for considering this important problem of situated political critique in a new way.

Beyond Persuasion

Looking to the rhetorical tradition, we find a more capacious understanding of rhetoric that goes beyond the dignity of persuasion. Such conceptions of rhetoric, as we will see, offer rich resources that sustain political critique. Where conceiving of rhetoric as "mere" persuasion has long been a hallmark of philosophy's valorization of reason alone, Ernesto Grassi's account of the rhetorical tradition redirects our attention to a much more productive and theoretically significant role, also originating with Cicero. Conceived of as an imaginative language, rhetoric in Grassi's understanding reaches far beyond its instrumental uses to encompass the creation of new meaning.[8] Such new meaning is not created in a vacuum but, rather, works creatively from within particular social and linguistic practices. In this way, rhetoric uniquely offers the capacity to develop new ways of thinking in response to contingent and novel circumstances and the changing needs of human life. Rhetoric provides indispensable resources for critique situated on the finite terrain of politics.

Insofar as we conceive of philosophy as proceeding by the force of logic to the exclusion or subordination of rhetoric and its play of imagination on the passions, our thought remains tethered to the first principles from which deduction follows. From where do we get the original insight into such first principles and what is the source for new models of thought? How, in other words, could we proceed beyond mere repetition with deduction alone? The discovery of the conditions of rational thought, Grassi argues, lies not in logic but in the imaginative power of figural language to generate new ways of ordering and presenting images on which speech that is both reasonable and effective depends. Metaphor and analogy are essential for generating new images and frameworks out of familiar terms. Such figural language entails a borrowing, or transfer, of familiar words into unfamiliar relation. to produce new meanings. It is, in other words, to discover or invent a new relation, not derived from fact or through logic, but by virtue of the ingenious activity of the speaker. This capacity of *ingenium*, a distinctive human ability for making meaning, works by joining the diverse and disparate. It "reveals something 'new' . . . something 'unexpected' and 'astonishing' by uncovering the 'similar in the unsimilar, i.e. what cannot be deduced rationally.'"[9] Understood this way, rhetoric does not simply adorn or destabilize philosophy's reasoned arguments; rather, it makes possible the production of new spaces for arguments and shared meaning.[10] As Grassi writes, "Insofar as metaphor has its root in the analogy between different things and makes this analogy immediately spring into 'sight,' it makes a fundamental contribution to the structure of our world."[11] To critically orient ourselves to the situated world of politics, rather than idealizing detachment, requires the creative power of rhetoric, unleashed through metaphor. Rhetoric as imaginative language is indispensable for envisioning our social and political arrangements in new and different ways.

To consider rhetoric as an indispensable capacity for critique then requires a shift in perspective from philosophical tradition. Always situated and dialogic, rhetoric presumes a particular audience, a relation between speaker and audience(s), located in a specific time and place.[12] The appeal to audience (or readers) may be explicit in the text or it may come by implication through the repetition of a familiar image or idiom. In both cases, the text marks its position within relations between speaker and audience. This situation invites us to read in new ways, even philosophical texts, attentive to what Mikhail Bakhtin calls heteroglossia.[13] To tend to this plurality of modes of speech within a text is to be aware that words and phrases, idioms and images, are not always deployed to produce and reproduce meaning in the same ways. Instead, we must tend to the moments when meanings are pluralized and decentered, following the play of style and argument and attuned to the possibility of language being deployed in new ways or even turned against itself, as in parody or satire. The presence of multiple and varied modes and forms of address does not necessarily mean that rhetoric has overtaken philosophy, undermining rational thought.[14] On the contrary, stylistic and figural invention, framed by the text's appeals to readers, can be recognized as contributing essentially to philosophical and political arguments themselves. Dialogic and heteroglossic dimensions of the text may challenge norms of philosophy's monologic forms of address. They can also, however, reveal the essential and transformative role of imaginative and inventive language in launching new modes of judgment and critique that lie at the heart of the philosophical enterprise.

Reconceiving Early Modern Rhetoric and Philosophy

Those who recount the seventeenth century as the end of the rhetorical tradition and the twin rise of the modern state and science are not without reason. Nowhere does the break seem clearer than in the philosophical and scientific innovations of the Royal Society, as recorded in Thomas Sprat's *History of the Royal Society*. The Royal Society counted among its members Locke, Hobbes, Robert Boyle, John Dryden, Isaac Newton, and others who, in Sprat's words, "have indeavor'd to separate the knowledge of Nature, from the colours of Rhetoric, the devices of Fancy, or the delightful deceit of Fables."[15] They professed "a close, naked, natural way of speaking; positive expressions, clear senses; a native easiness: bringing all things as near the Mathematical plainness, as they can: and preferring the language of Artizans, Countrymen, and Merchants, before that, of Wits, or Scholars."[16] Contrasted with the "Artifice, Humors, and Passions of Sects," Sprat presents the emerging natural philosophy, with its plain style, as conducive to political stability and religious moderation.[17] We need think only of Hobbes's *Leviathan*, in which a new science of politics draws upon mathematical reasoning and institutes sovereign control over linguistic creativity and interpretation, to see how closely interwoven with politics these developments in science, philosophy, and language were.

Locke enjoys a central role in these momentous changes and it takes no stretch of imagination to associate him with the "rhetoric against rhetoric." He is aligned with the Royal Society, in tension with older traditions of Aristotelianism and humanism, on the one hand, and new, nonconformist religious sects, on the other. In contrast to Hobbes, however, Locke's New Science is that the early English empirical scientists. Locke does not write extensively on rhetoric per se, but when he does, there is little doubt that he too harbors suspicions of the capacity of language to create confusion in the human understanding and conflict in social and political life. In his best-known passage on rhetoric, Locke speaks with great consternation of the relationship of rhetoric to passions, and to judgment, while advocating for order and clarity in speech. If we are to "speak of Things as they are, we must allow, that all the Art of Rhetoric, besides Order and Clearness, all the artificial and figurative application of Words Eloquence hath invented, are for nothing else but to insinuate wrong *Ideas*, move the Passions, and thereby mislead the Judgment; and so indeed are perfect cheat: And therefore, however laudable or allowable Oratory may render them in Harangues and popular Addresses, they are certainly, in all Discourses that pretend to inform or instruct, wholly to be avoided" (3.10.34).[18] Rhetoric matters for Locke here, insofar as it raises the power of the passions to overwhelm judgment. It raises, in other words, a fundamental concern for his philosophy.

Not surprisingly, then, figural language comes under his critical gaze in several texts, especially those concerned with the cultivation and conduct of the human understanding, including but not limited to *An Essay Concerning Human Understanding*. He speaks of rhetoric at times in a pejorative manner, casting it in feminine form, "the fair Sex" (3.10.34), and emphasizing its ornamental role of language: "Nor do I deny, that those Words, and the like, are to have their place in the common use of Languages, that have made them currant. It looks like too much affectation wholly to lay them by: and Philosophy, it self, though it likes not a gaudy dress, yet when it appears in publick, must have so much Complacency, as to be cloathed in the ordinary Fashion and Language of the Country, so far as it can consist with Truth and Perspicuity" (2.21.20). He positions judgment as "a way of proceeding quite contrary to Metaphor and Allusion, wherein for the most part, lies that entertainment and pleasantry of Wit, which strikes so lively on the Fancy, and therefor so acceptable to all People" (2.11.2). The beauty of such figural language requires "no labour of thought, to examine what Truth or Reason there is in it," Locke complains, thereby building his reputation as hostile not only to rhetoric but also to aesthetics more generally. In *Of the Conduct of the Understanding*, written for possible inclusion in the *Essay*, he recognizes the need for figural language but seems to reserve only a secondary place for it: "Figured and metaphorical expressions do well to illustrate more abstruse and unfamiliar ideas which the mind is not yet thoroughly accustomed to; but then they must be made use of to illustrate ideas that we already have, not to paint to us those which we yet have not. Such borrowed and allusive ideas may follow real and solid truth, to set it off when found, but must by no means be set in its place and taken for it."[19] In *Some Thoughts Concerning Education*, which sets out a plan for cultivating reason in young gentlemen, he argues that right reasoning "does not consist in talking in *mode* and *figure* itself" and seeks to excise from the curriculum the "art and formality of disputing" as well as formal rules of rhetoric.[20] In the educational writings, as in philosophy, the call for clarity in speech rings throughout, as does the concern that the persuasive power of language carries the potential to undermine proper modes of conduct of the understanding (*STCE*, §189). For "[t]he Mind without looking any farther, rests satisfied with the agreeableness of the Picture, and the gayety of the Fancy: And it is a kind of an affront to go about to examine it, by the severe Rules of Truth, and good Reason" (2.11.2).

Representing an extreme case of rhetoric as a challenge to reason is the case of enthusiasts, where the effects are felt in moral and political matters. Enthusiasm, Locke argues, entails the replacement of reason with fancy, or imagination, when authority is granted on the basis of passion rather than evidence. For those moved by such inwardly felt religious passions, according to Locke, "Reason is lost upon them, they are above it: they see the Light infused into their Understandings, and cannot be mistaken; 'tis clear and visible there, like the Light of bright Sunshine, shews it self, and needs no other Proof, but its own Evidence: they feel the Hand of GOD moving them within, and the impulses of the Spirit, and cannot be mistaken in what they feel" (4.19.8). What they see and feel, however, is not sensory experience, but metaphor and simile, Locke argues: "[T]hey are sure, because they are sure: and their Perswasions are right, only because they are strong in them. For, when what they say is strip'd of the Metaphor of seeing and feeling, this is all it amounts to: and yet these Similes so impose on them, that they serve them for certainty in themselves, and demonstration to others" (4.19.9). In enthusiasm, rhetorical figure and imagination undermine cautious judgment based on evidence.

What reason is there to suspect that anything more is needed to explain this apparent break between Locke's philosophy and rhetoric, in keeping with the tenor of his times? There are clues even in these few passages that something more complicated is going on. First, in rejecting disputation and the formal rules of rhetoric in education, Locke rejects only certain institutionalized practices and objects of the rhetorical tradition while reinforcing the importance of writing and speaking well. Where handbooks of rhetoric fall short, examples of eloquent and effective speech are much more powerful. A favored example for speech and letters is none other than Cicero (*STCE*, §189). Second, figures such as metaphor and simile maintain at least some useful, if conscribed, role in communicating ideas, even, or rather especially, the ineffable concepts of philosophy. This suggests the possibility that reason alone may not be sufficient in all cases. Finally, when

Locke turns a critical eye on rhetoric, his concerns are often rooted in questions of authority and practices of judgment. Establishing authority and making judgments are hardly removed from the traditional terrain of rhetoric. Locke's concerns about rhetoric are motivated by the very issues that the rhetorical tradition put at the center: questions of authority and judgment.

There are deeper reasons to question the epic tale of rupture between philosophy, science, and rhetoric in the seventeenth century in general, and in Locke's work in particular. Large-scale transformations such as these are rarely so sudden or discrete. Rather, rhetoric, philosophy, and science come together in unexpected ways in this creative period of transformation, challenging us to conceive of these relationships in fuller and more nuanced ways. While the phrase "the rhetoric against rhetoric" acknowledges that the castigation of rhetoric does not necessarily signal its exile, the phrase resists the richer and more nuanced meanings afforded by the rhetorical tradition. Interpreters of Hobbes, for example, have closely examined his shifting and complex engagements with rhetoric and the rhetorical tradition to find resources well beyond the negative and instrumental uses highlighted by Garsten and others. As Victoria Kahn shows, Hobbes's claims against rhetoric must be understood as unfolding within a sophisticated rhetorical engagement between author and reader, in which the reader's assent is solicited from the outset to an analogy between the self and the text's presentation of a new political subjectivity. Leviathan's social contract, in which interpretive as well as political power are granted to the sovereign, is premised on a prior linguistic agreement: a metaphoric contract concerning the mode of reading both self and text. Moreover, it is precisely Hobbes's concerns with humans in a materialist world, as embodied and imaginative creatures driven by passions, that makes rhetoric dangerous but also indispensable.[21] This is not to ignore Hobbes's challenge to authoritative ideas and texts of the rhetorical tradition or his wariness of the individual capacity for judgment. Rather it is a signal that rhetoric was not so easily dispensed with by early modern thinkers, despite their criticisms. This is especially the case for those theorists, like Hobbes as well as Locke, who sought to legitimate and challenge claims to authority in new ways.

Closer examination of Sprat and the New Scientists also reveals that rhetoric both sustained the claims of the New Science as well as serving as object of attack. As they challenged traditional modes of epistemic credibility, natural scientists needed to garner authority for their new modes of philosophical and scientific claim-making. Early empirical scientists rejected the principle of authority of Aristotelianism and humanism in exchange for their own claims to knowledge based in experience. Brian Vickers shows how the attacks on rhetoric represented by Sprat's *History* do not mark such a profound break between a victorious anti-rhetoric camp against a losing rhetorical tradition or sect.[22] Rather, a seemingly generalized hostility to rhetoric can indicate not so much an epistemological commitment as a commonplace of contentious political arguments. The New Scientists "were not against language, or rhetoric, or the imagination. They were against their opponents' misuse of them—or, perhaps more simply, they were against their opponents."[23] Making accusations of the abuse of rhetoric in these highly charged political and philosophical debates is not the same as rejecting rhetoric, certainly not in practice, but not even necessarily in principle.

Language was a deep concern for the New Science and drove linguistic innovation in a number of disparate directions, including in Bacon's advocacy of analogy and aphorism as well as John Wilkins's universal language.[24] Sprat's insistence on a plain style, like Locke's call for order and clarity is not a rejection of rhetoric as such, but a call for one rhetorical style over another.[25] The innovations in natural science also led New Scientists to turn to nature as an abundant source for new analogies, spurring on "a free use of rhetoric, both of figures . . . and tropes (especially metaphor)."[26] While Sprat cautions against "Rhetorical Flourishes" in Royal Society reports, he writes that the language of the New Science must "represent *Truth*, cloth'd with Bodies; and to bring *Knowledg* back again to our very Senses, from whence it was at first deriv'd to our understandings."[27] In other words, Sprat calls upon the language to make vivid its experimental findings, recalling the rhetorical tradition's notion of *enargeia*.[28] While accusations of the abuse of rhetoric intensified, style and figure remained integral to the philosophical pursuits of the New Science, not as mere ornament but in the creation of new methods for asserting and assessing truth claims.

These more nuanced and complex accounts of rhetoric in the work of Hobbes and the New Science signal the inadequacy of "the rhetoric against rhetoric" to capture the relation of rhetoric to these philosophical, scientific, and political transformations. Locke, however, differs in significant ways from both Hobbes and Sprat. Sprat rightly does not enjoy the philosophical significance of Locke or Hobbes and Sprat's *History* is guided by practical goals of generating support for the Royal Society from church and state. Hobbes takes on (in both senses of the phrase) the rhetorical tradition in more obvious and extended ways than does Locke. Moreover, Hobbes launched a powerful critique of prevailing political assumptions, but he actively sought to obstruct such a critical sensibility in individuals. In substance and in style, examining the role of rhetoric in Locke's philosophical and political thought poses a different set of challenges and possibilities. His engagement with rhetoric is less obvious, to begin with. However, his particular interest in resistance to authority makes his work an even more important site in which to consider the relationship of rhetoric to political critique. To do so is to consider political critique not only as practiced by the theorist but also as theorized as a capacity of the individual and the political community.

In light of these challenges, it is not surprising that the attention given to Locke's relationship to rhetoric, albeit limited, primarily focuses on his comments in the *Essay* and usually arises as a question for philosophy rather than for politics, though one more often raised by literary scholars than by philosophers. Locke's claim that knowledge comes from experience in the *Essay* is taken as the basis for an apparent hostility to rhetoric cast as a wayward and disruptive influence on the understanding. These positions, furthermore, have been construed as evidence of his "apparent indifference, and presumed hostility, towards the realm of the aesthetic," discouraging further inquiry into his rhetorical engagements.[29]

An important exception to this is Paul de Man's essay "The Epistemology of Metaphor," in which he opens the question of rhetoric in Locke's *Essay* in new ways by pointing to the abundance of figural language, including metaphor, personification, and catachresis, in the writing of this supposed enemy of the aesthetic. Locke's theory of language, he argues, cannot constrain itself to a basis in unmediated sensory perception but, rather, is enacted as a theory of tropes.[30] For de Man recognition of the figural character of Lockean language attests to the failure of his philosophical project to free the rational subject from the influence of rhetoric. Locke, on this reading, is still understood as hostile to rhetoric and the aesthetic more generally even as the evidence of a more complicated relation of rhetoric to his philosophy mounts.[31]

My central claim in this book is not simply that Locke's writings have a rhetorical character, or that, by necessity, no text can evade its rhetorical dimensions. While such claims are important, my contention is that Locke's use of rhetoric is not an accidental lapse but rather is constitutive of his theory and practice of critique. To consider the productive role of rhetoric in philosophy, in general, requires that we read a theorist like Locke in unaccustomed ways, but we can and should do more. We must read Locke, in particular, with attention to his style as a matter of philosophical interest, not just as a counterpart or competitor to his theoretical argument. Put somewhat differently, I contend that it is inadequate to read Locke's philosophical and political texts without a consideration of how his style indispensably contributes to the arguments therein. As I will argue, Locke's central focus on experience in his *Essay* requires the capacity for invention to generate critical purchase on individual, philosophical, social, and political norms and practices. Both experience and invention, as we will see, are necessary for Locke's conception of moral, natural, and political philosophy.

Rhetoric and Locke's Political Theory

If Locke's philosophy is seen as hostile to rhetoric, his political thought appears to take no note of it whatsoever. There are at least two reasons for this perception. First, the political concepts for which Locke is best known—the state of nature, social contract, and natural rights—evidence his interest in a critical vantage point that looks beyond existing social and political institutions and practices, in order to open them to revision. Insofar as these concepts are seen in terms of a retreat from the historical, customary, and affective relations that give shape to particular political communities, Locke's thought is then construed, by critics and admirers alike, as rationalist and ahistorical. This is not only to suggest that Locke is taken as a theorist for whom reason is an important capacity of the individual but also, and much more strongly, to associate him with rationalism, broadly construed.

To say that Locke has been associated with rationalism, in a broad sense, is not to ignore his identification with the empiricist tradition. Rather, the Lockean subject, cast as the "man of reason," is premised on the valorization of reason as the sole faculty of critique.[32] The term *man of reason* also indicates detachment from embodied social differences of class, gender, and race as well as the social and psychological effects of passions, imagination, and language. This is particularly resonant when Locke is taken up, as he so often is, as a founding figure of the liberal tradition. His seminal place in the empiricist tradition of philosophy does not necessarily diminish this image of reason's operating independently of other faculties, such as imagination or language, and without social or material influence, whether corporeal, historical, or economic. Such an appeal to a position external to politics and society can be construed as a source of unyielding rigor for criticism of established practices and norms. For others, such detachment sustains only certain claims to political critique and resistance while maintaining blindness to other forms of inequality and subjection, especially those attached to social and economic status.[33] While there is considerable disagreement on the merits of such an external standpoint for critique, these different interpretations concur in their perception of Locke's political thought as one of rationalist detachment. Such an elevation of reason alone seems perfectly concordant with the exclusion or subordination of rhetoric.

Second, Locke's major texts, both political and philosophical, have often struck readers as discontinuous, repetitive, and plagued by inconsistency. Indeed, we might expect a theorist with Locke's reputation to offer more straightforward, concise, and consistent philosophical treatments. Yet among Locke's major works we find the long, rambling, and circular manner of *An Essay Concerning Human Understanding* as well as the *First Treatise,* widely reputed more for its redundant, long-winded, and polemical attacks than for its theoretical merit.[34] Even the *Second Treatise* requires careful partitioning out of certain chapters to preserve the brief, conceptual framework from the unruly examples and arguments that seem to undermine the abstract rationality of the social contract. There is something that does not seem to sit right between the style and the substance of Locke's thought.

In response to such impressions, interpreters have long organized his work and ideas along dichotomies of rationalist and empiricist, theoretical and polemical, fact and fiction in order to make sense of these problems of style and logic.[35] The most famous, but hardly the last, of such claims is Peter Laslett's depiction of Locke as "perhaps the least consistent of all the great philosophers" for the incompatibility of his appeals to natural law in the *Two Treatises* and his thoroughgoing critique of innate ideas in the *Essay.*[36] Declaring that his thought is riven helps to make sense of our exasperation as readers as well as our philosophical disappointments. Moreover, such partitioning relieves late modern readers of the interpretive dilemmas of Lockean writing that evidently plague us.

It is not the goal of this book to heal such divisions and recover a unitary Locke. Rather, I question the widespread sense that Locke's repetitions and discontinuities mark a failure of both rhetoric and philosophy, that they pose a problem in need of a solution. Locke's thought may be riven; indeed, it may be fractured into an even greater plurality than Laslett and others have suspected. That does not mean it must conform to familiar dichotomous lines that separate philosophy from rhetoric, experience from reason, and matter from language.[37] On the contrary, Locke's repetitions and discontinuities signal a question of style—that is to say, of rhetoric—that too often goes unasked, most of all with regard to his political writings. To engage rather than partition out, or make exception of, these repetitions and discontinuities requires that we inquire anew into the relationship of philosophy to rhetoric in Locke's thought. Locke's reputation as a theorist of a masterful rationality and abstract individualism stands uneasily alongside the style of his texts. It is this uneasiness that invites my inquiry.

To consider the role of rhetoric in Locke's work is to challenge some of our most familiar images of the thinker, not least in his capacity as political theorist. Where a rhetorical stance suggests a writer engaged with particular audiences, Locke is traditionally praised as well as castigated for looking beyond the particular polity to abstract states of nature and social compacts. Contextualist readers of Locke have shown the way in which his writings can be understood as interventions in specific political controversies, such as the Exclusion Crisis. They have shown the way in which Locke, even in his most abstract utterances, engages in and contends with particular debates and vocabularies of his time and place, whether acknowledged by the author or not.[38] While they are enriching, particularly for their challenge to all-too-familiar depictions of Locke as a precociously secular, liberal, individualist thinker, such accounts deemphasize the plural and disruptive uses of language that rhetoric enables. It is worth noting, however, that historically inflected interpretations of Locke reveal him to have been deeply engaged with matters of the pulpit and the political stage. From his early education and academic appointment as a lecturer in rhetoric to his later political and religious concerns, Locke was immersed in contexts in which rhetoric was of supreme importance.[39] Why then do we not consider more seriously and more often the role of rhetoric in Locke's political theory?

Situating Political Critique

Locke's famous claim in the *Essay* that all knowledge comes from experience places him as a founding figure in the empiricist tradition, in which experience operates as a firm foundation for rational thought that is external to human cognition, concepts, and normative frameworks. Caught up with such a "myth of the given," Locke's thought has long been criticized for its naive faith in unmediated sense perception and the way it obscures the need for normative concepts and language to make experience meaningful. This is not the only way to understand Lockean experience, however. Theorists and historians of literature and rhetoric as well as of science have greatly expanded our understanding of the relation of rhetoric to experience in the early modern period. In ways that both challenge and extend de Man's insights, they show that despite well-known attacks on rhetoric, proponents of the New Science developed a new relation to rhetoric rather than fully abandoning it. The valuing of experience itself is shared by both the rhetorical tradition and the natural philosophy that interested Locke, troubling their opposition. To be sure, the concept of experience underwent significant transformation in this period, but it can also be seen as common, if contested, ground for these two supposedly antithetical traditions. Moreover, Locke's *Essay* plays an important role in this period of transformation.

I approach Locke's claim to experience through the early modern revival of Epicurean materialism, which emphasizes a chastened practice of probable judgment based on persuasive evidence and testimony rather than on certain foundations. While a number of scholars have noted in Locke's thought the influence of Pierre Gassendi, the philosopher of early modern Epicureanism, rarely have they considered how this might require us to reconsider the traditional assumption of Locke's hostility to rhetoric.[40] More than just an epistemology, Epicurean materialism involved "an entire symbolic cultural mode," requiring rhetoric no less than epistemology.[41] Rhetoric, in other words, is not unequivocally excluded by the major scientific and philosophical shifts of the seventeenth century. In more subtle forms, it was essential for challenging and asserting authority, both epistemic and social, in new ways. Read through the empiricist tradition and its critics, Lockean experience remains captured within a stark opposition between mind and world, self and others. With Epicurean materialism, it becomes possible to see how the claim to experience acquires meaning and critical force only when it is combined with the inventive capacities of rhetoric. Recognizing the importance of this Epicurean materialist background rightly trains our attention on the importance of experience for Lockean judgment, but without losing sight of the indispensable role of rhetorical invention as a capacity for gaining critical purchase on existing norms and practices.

It is not my intention to place Locke formally within the rhetorical tradition as a primary intellectual influence. Rather, with this expanded understanding of the importance of rhetoric to philosophy and to critique, we will be well positioned to consider in new ways Locke's nuanced and conflicted relationship to rhetoric and its significance for his theory and practice of critique. To be sure, Locke criticizes eloquent speech. Looking beyond these charges of "mere" persuasion, however, opens up a variety of modes in which rhetoric can sustain theoretical and political argument: as figure and trope, satire and parody, exemplar and fable, and most of all, ingenious, inventive activity. Being attuned to the creative and theoretical contributions of these rhetorical gestures will generate new possibilities concerning the rhetorical and critical significance of particular figures of femininity and foreignness, recurring in Locke's writings, that Locke's admirers too often ignore and critics view solely as an impediment. At the center of those critical engagements with authority, we find Locke's figures and tropes— his exemplary mothers, fathers, cannibals, and Indians—productive of new political meaning and possibilities out of particular images. The place of such imaginative language and unexpected stylizing within Locke's theoretical writing will open up onto the role of inventive activity in giving meaning and force to his critique of philosophical and political authority.

In drawing attention to the importance of invention in Locke's philosophical and political writings, I invoke the word, invention, for its capacity to bridge the literary, philosophical, scientific, and political realms in a manner appropriate to his wide-ranging modes of inquiry. The *Oxford English Dictionary* defines this word in rhetorical terms as indicating the finding or discovering of arguments and topics. In scientific terms, it refers, as is common today, to the creation of a new instrument or idea. In literature, music, and poetry, and even with regard to political institutions, *invention* can be used to speak of a fabrication or contrivance, that is, of the creative work of humans. The wide scope of invention bridges the realms of fiction and fact, aesthetic and rational, creation and discovery. It includes creation ex nihilo as well as the language of finding, which may refer to that lodged in the memory or hidden within nature. To speak of inventive activity is not necessarily to depart from reality, either into fantasy or to the Archimedean point. Nor is it necessarily to work reproductively with materials already given, whether natural, social, or human. Invention encompasses the distinctive human capacity to work creatively from a position situated in natural, social, historical, linguistic, and political contexts. That may involve radical creativity as well as simple recollection, or some combination of the two. It is precisely this resistance to the dichotomies of rationalist philosophy that enables us to envision our social and political practices in new ways, that is, to launch and sustain situated political critique.

As Grassi reminds us, for Cicero, such inventive activity was the means by which humans transformed the given world into a meaningful realm, a distinctive mode of work always situated within social and political relations.[42] The rhetorical tradition thus recalls us to the originary role of inventive labor in making and transforming the world from within its particular shared practices and traditions, without necessarily reproducing them. Broadly speaking, Locke shares this Ciceronian interest in human labor enacted upon nature as an originary source for politics.[43] As we will see, for Locke, human workmanship extends also to the generation of words and ideas from experience. It is in Locke's emphasis on human activity and judgment that we will discover the fundamental role of rhetoric. To identify such human activity with labor is not to exclude the role of invention. Rather, it is to recognize the productive and creative role of invention in the indispensable *work of rhetoric*.

Using Epicurean materialism as a vantage point on Locke's thought, I offer a close examination of the two most significant works written by Locke, *An Essay Concerning Human Understanding* and the *Two Treatises of Government*, to reveal the ways in which rhetoric and experience are essential to his critique of authority in philosophy and politics. In considering these two texts, we go to the source of Locke's reputation for hostility to rhetoric and imagination and his reputation for both rationalism in politics and empiricism in philosophy. The choice of these two of Locke's works should not be taken as a sign that they are the only texts that reveal the significance of rhetoric to critique or that they are the only ones carrying significance for political theory and philosophy. Quite to the contrary, Locke was a prolific writer, and I believe that the dynamics of rhetoric and experience in his thought echo throughout his writings in various and interesting ways. I have chosen these two for their outsized significance for scholars of political theory, philosophy, and literature. Further, they are particularly rich for their insights into Lockean critique because of the extended engagement with questions of judgment. For this reason, I begin my exploration of the inventive nature of Lockean critique with these two classics. Such a beginning should be understood as an invitation rather than a conclusion to the powerful work of rhetoric to be found elsewhere in Locke's thought.

We begin, in Chapter 2, by revisiting Locke's well-known claim to experience, as the basis for his long-standing reputation as an empiricist and by extension his hostility to rhetoric. Whereas this claim has traditionally been situated within a historical narrative that charts a sharp break in the seventeenth century, marking the decline of the rhetorical tradition and the rise of the New Science, I resituate Locke in a more nuanced and overlapping contact zone between rhetoric and science, or natural philosophy. Understanding Locke's situation within the early modern revival of Epicurean materialism allows us to take his interest in experience seriously without rushing to attribute to him a naive and untenable foundationalism in unmediated sense perception. As we will see, two important implications follow from this shift. First, Locke's notion of reason is rooted in probable judgment rather than certainty. This notion of judgment as a qualitative weighing of evidence and testimony places Locke at the intersection of rhetorical and legal tradition, on the one hand, and a new empirical science, on the other. Locke figures centrally in the reworking of experience from the realm of rhetoric and politics to a new philosophy with judgment at its center. Second, Epicurean materialism acknowledged the essential role of rhetoric, in contrast to the Cartesian and Spinozan hostility to language. Recognizing Locke's Epicurean materialism opens up new ways of exploring a productive relationship between experience and rhetoric that are obscured by reading back into his work a latter-day empiricism. In examining the claim to experience through this lens, however, we gain a deeper sense of the challenges that Locke sets up for himself in grounding judgment in moral and natural philosophy, in experience.

Chapter 3 examines Locke's negotiation of the problem of judgment that follows from his claim to experience. This chapter reveals most vividly Locke's relationship of both debt and denial to the rhetorical tradition. Experience for Locke becomes the basis for reasonable judgment, but also a source of error, caused by imaginative and passionate excess. Locating this problem of judgment at the center of the *Essay*, I argue that Locke's well-known anxiety about the passionate force of rhetoric is uneasily but significantly combined with his reappropriation of rhetoric for his critique of timeless, universal claims to truth. Whether in science, religion, or politics, we will see how, for Locke, even the most abstract and universal concepts emerge from particular experience. Sensory experience alone is not enough to give us the normative purchase or the passionate force needed for good judgment, however. So Locke turns to rhetoric—to analogies, metaphors, and personification—for the invention of his most cherished concepts out of ordinary experience. Rhetoric's capacity to impart new meaning through vivid figures and tropes is essential to his account of concepts (both moral and scientific) and language. Locke, however, reassigns rhetorical capacities from the orator to the individual participant in ordinary speech. In a sense, he democratizes the inventive and forceful possibilities of rhetorical speech. I contend that Locke articulates a critical capacity, shared by all, to reinvent words and ideas, that is, to critically reinterpret human experience.

In chapters 4 and 5, I show how this novel account of Lockean critique transforms the meaning of Locke's political thought. Chapter 4 takes a new look at the infamously repetitive refutation of patriarchal authority in the *First Treatise*. What has been dismissed as redundant preoccupation with minutiae is rather Locke's transformation of a timeless political universal—that of patriarchalism. Identifying in Locke's repetitions a rhetorical strategy, I draw out the deep affinities between the critical project of the *Essay* and the *First Treatise*, in that both seek to unseat claims to timeless universal truths. Locke unexpectedly emerges as a creative and forceful challenger not only to the political claims of patriarchalists but also to a larger symbolic order of interwoven images of familial and political authority. In tracing Locke's use of feminine and foreign figures, we find that Lockean critique works because, not in spite of, the pluralization of meaning and the turning of language against itself. Such a thorough transformation of a symbolic political order could not be achieved by logic alone, and indeed, the force of Locke's text is lost on those looking only for its logic. My emphasis on the formative role of rhetoric and experience reveals a creative strategy of reinventing the familiar terms of patriarchalist politics. With figure and trope, satire and parody, Locke turns the language of patriarchal order against itself. In other words, rhetoric sustains Locke's devastating critique as it proceeds from within the very social and political discourse that he challenges.

In chapter 5, I take up the challenge of showing how Locke's debt to rhetoric matters for his classic theory of consent and resistance in the *Second Treatise*. Does the rhetorical reinvention of experience that challenges claims to authority in the *Essay* and *First Treatise* contribute positively to Locke's political vision? I argue that it must. The normative force of the *Second Treatise* depends upon the capacity to instill the conviction that political authority comes from acts of consent rather than the immemorial rule of father-kings. This counterintuitive task is not achieved through the mere assertion of a concept of consent. Rather, Locke seeks to shift the terms of familiar experience with his political anthropology, a series of examples and stories usually accorded secondary status. He recounts a familiar past of fatherlike kings as a story of consent. In recurring versions of this story, he presents this past from increasingly plural perspectives. Readers witness as Locke successively reconstructs their political past as tales of judgment based on experience and a recent, but reversible, loss of freedom. Through these successive recollections of the past, the anthropology reawakens dulled political sensibilities to a memory of freedom and the possibility of founding anew. The chapter offers a significant reversal of the received interpretation that the abstract and universal concepts alone provide the normative force of Lockean critique. Instead of breaking with the past, Locke reinvents contingent political experience to generate new horizons of political possibility. Lockean critique, in this way, emerges from the familiar ground of political experience to inventively reimagine the political past and present so as to generate futures that could be otherwise.

In the conclusion, we come back to Locke's reputation for masterful reason and his association with what James Tully calls the "empire of uniformity" of modern constitutionalism.[44] The central place of rhetorical invention in Lockean critique, however, suggests a very different legacy for his thought. It is not a flight from the material and contingent conditions of political thought that Lockean critique requires; rather, Locke draws inventively from political experience to generate normative force. The past does not always obviously offer the resources for critical purchase on the present that we seek and that is why invention is essential for generating new critical vantage points. It is thus not detachment from our shared political situations, but rather an inventive relation to our past and present, that brings into sight possibilities for new political futures. Locke emerges as an exemplary political theorist for transcending the received opposition between rhetoric and philosophy and its problem of situated political critique. It is not hard to find more engaging writers than Locke, not to mention more powerful orators, poets, or preachers—it is not, in other words, his rhetoric alone that sets him apart. Rather, it is the way that he integrates rhetorical capacities into a newly articulated philosophical and political subject, bestowed with the capability and obligation of judgment. From this reinvention of rhetorical and philosophical tradition, Locke derives rich resources for thinking in new ways about democratic practices of critique, however much late modern democracy may exceed the limits of his own theoretical imagination.

2

THE CLAIM TO EXPERIENCE

Whence comes it by that vast store, which the busy and boundless Fancy of Man has painted on it, with an almost endless variety? Whence has it all the materials of Reason and Knowledge? To this I answer, in one word, From *Experience*: In that, all our Knowledge is founded; and from that it ultimately derives it self.

—*An Essay Concerning Human Understanding*, 2.1.2

With these opening words to book 2 of *An Essay Concerning Human Understanding*, Locke makes his well-known claim that all knowledge comes from experience. This claim has situated Locke as a founding figure in the British empiricist tradition, inaugurating a lineage continued by Berkeley and Hume. While early modern empiricism finds few champions today, it is not uncommon to see interpreters reiterate depictions of the *Essay* as entangled in the intractable problems posed by belief in a certain foundation in sense perception and an accompanying hostility to language, especially in its imaginative, rhetorical forms. Locke's *Essay* has long been the target of criticisms directed against empiricism as positing an untenable faith in the mind as tabula rasa, a blank slate as passive receptor for sensory impressions, independent of and prior to both normative frameworks and language. Identified with what Wilfred Sellars calls the "myth of the given," Locke's claim to experience is seen as providing a secure foundation for human knowledge and reason in a precognitive, prelinguistic conception of sensory perception.[1] Such a faith in unmediated sense perception depends on a dualist split between mind and world, self and others. It draws, in Richard Rorty's words, a "veil of ideas" that insulates the rational and self-certain subject from a shared world that is constituted through social practices, particularly language.[2] While contemporary readers may be skeptical of empiricism's naive foundationalism and unyielding dualism, Locke's supposed antipathy to language, especially rhetoric, remains an article of faith.[3]

Scholarship examining the historical context leading up to and surrounding Locke's *Essay* offers a number reasons to loosen the hold of Locke's image as founding figure of British empiricism. The labeling of Locke as an empiricist, Hans Aarsleff suggests, owes more to nineteenth-century histories of philosophies than to the *Essay* itself.[4] Such latter-day labels give way to more focused attention on Locke's involvement with seventeenth-century science, under the influence of Francis Bacon and Robert Boyle, and on his moral concerns that are framed by a Christian cosmology. In James Farr's words, "The alleged empiricist philosopher of common sense has had restored to him an epistemology devoted to vindicating its theocentric framework and an understanding of the scope and methods of science."[5] To contextualize Locke's *Essay* in this way, however, does not necessarily eliminate the association between Locke and those criticisms launched against empiricism. Charles Taylor, for example, draws from Tully's study to emphasize the theological commitments of Locke's thought. For Taylor, Locke's subject achieves this very dualist stance, namely, its radical detachment from the shared social world, through a firm foundation in Christian theology. Locke's "punctual self" needs more than experience to achieve self-certainty, yet such recognition does not necessarily trouble his reputed hostility to social and linguistic practices.[6]

Locke's claim to experience is indeed the launching pad for the theory of knowledge and language offered up by the *Essay Concerning Human Understanding*. Dislodging this claim from its latter-day legacy in empiricism's privileging of unmediated sense perception, untouched by language and concepts, opens up an alternative understanding of Locke's claim to experience as a critical project, emerging against a backdrop of significant developments in early modern philosophy, science, and rhetoric together. In this chapter, we will resituate the claim to experience and its relationship to rhetoric in two ways. First, Locke's claim to experience emerged in a historical moment marked by a productive breakdown, rather than enmity, between philosophical-scientific practice and the rhetorical tradition. Second, that breakdown was integral to a culture of Epicurean materialism, in which Locke participated and that marks the style and substance of his writing. As we will see, readers of Locke who emphasize both his theological and scientific commitments cite the influence of the early modern Epicureanism of Gassendi, which helps to disentangle Locke from a latter-day empiricism and its philosophical dilemmas. In its place, Locke emerges as a theorist of judgment rather than certainty, negotiating a world conceived in terms of ineliminable contingency and uncertainty. Most important, this modern Epicureanism takes up the project of cultivating judgment in a manner that preserves a key role for rhetoric. We will then be able to recognize Locke's appeal to experience as one that engages contingency, affective attachment, and imaginative language to critique existing authority and reconceive the subject.

Experience: Between Philosophy and Rhetoric

The familiar opposition between philosophy and rhetoric and between language and the material world structures a classic tale about Locke and the seventeenth century as a moment of rupture that starts to fray upon closer examination of a growing interest in experience and probable judgment. Locke's relationship with the Royal Society and his lifelong passion for natural philosophical inquiries testify to the importance of scientific pursuits in his life and work.[7] This association might seem to reinforce the view of a scientifically oriented Locke as hostile or indifferent to rhetoric. Histories of science and rhetoric, however, paint a more nuanced picture.

Claims to experience made by Locke and his scientific cohort emerge, not from an opposition between rhetoric and philosophy, but from a weakening of this divide. The notion of experience underwent a significant transformation in Locke's lifetime. Experience, construed as part of the contingent world of appearances, was traditionally located on the side of the rhetorical tradition against Aristotelian philosophy's search for demonstrative certainty and the forms of nature. Logic and rhetoric were sorted by a division of labor, with each assigned to different arenas of knowledge and action. Knowledge claims proceeded by deduction from certain principles, limiting credibility for the contingent observations of natural philosophy or other claims based in experience. On the other side of this divide, rhetoric related to questions of opinion and belief proper to the realms of politics, law, literature, and religion.[8] In England, rhetoric, especially Ciceronian, had been taught since the Middle Ages as part of the curriculum, alongside grammar and logic, at Oxford and Cambridge.[9]

By the sixteenth century, Renaissance humanism had recovered and accorded new value to the category of experience while working to discredit scholastic philosophy.[10] Reformers such as Rodolphus Agricola, Philipp Melanchthon, and

Petrus Ramus offered various ways of reworking the categories of rhetoric and dialectic, such that logical arguments made from plausible, uncertain premises became appropriate for all areas of study.[11] Different versions of a new dialectic emerged, taking over probable reasoning from rhetoric. Agricola, influential for both Melanchthon and Ramus, helped bring about "a semantic revolution" by redefining dialectic in manner that, somewhat paradoxically, reclaimed the Ciceronian view of invention as a rhetorical activity.[12] In other words, Agricola's new dialectic took over from rhetoric the inventive capacity to generate topics and probable arguments on both sides of a question, *in utramque partem*. English rhetorics from 1530s onward by Henry Peacham, Thomas Wilson, and others show the marks of Agricola's and Melanchthon's influence, in particular. Influential on the Continent and for Calvinist Protestants in England, Ramus offered a subsequent reform of dialectic that promised certainty rather than plausible arguments on both sides, breaking with the controversialist tradition. Invention, nonetheless, remains on the side of dialectic for Ramus, while rhetoric is reduced to style and delivery. Rather than there being a decline of rhetoric, the modes of inquiry associated with dialectic come increasingly to draw upon those previously assigned to rhetoric in order to more deeply engage the realm of experience.[13] These humanists lowered the divide between philosophy and rhetoric over the course of the sixteenth century. They expanded their modes of inquiry and respect for experience-based knowledge into the natural sciences. As Barbara Shapiro explains, "The wall that for centuries had separated philosophy from rhetoric, reason from experience, and certainty from probability crumbled still further as a number of humanists attempted to develop unified arts of discourse that rearranged and combined elements of logic, dialectic, and rhetoric."[14]

With these reforms and a growing disenchantment with the earlier distinction between science and rhetoric, there was no longer a particular mode of discourse appropriate to scientific inquiry. The seventeenth century witnessed an increasing dissatisfaction with this breakdown of boundaries , alongside the continued erosion of the credibility of the older order. In response, efforts arose to articulate modes of truth claiming that aspired to a higher standard than humanist claims to plausibility while responding to the skepticism that worked to discredit Scholastic claims to certainty.[15] At the same time, the contentious politics of the Reformation and Counter-Reformation sparked a more intense interest in rhetoric as an affective and motivational force.[16] Responding to these manifold pressures and frustrations, New Scientists of the seventeenth century yet again reconceived relations between philosophy, rhetoric, and experience. Some, like Descartes, recommitted themselves to demonstrative certainty in the wake of radical skepticism, while Hobbes offered up his new science of politics focused on the passions, using mathematical reasoning and definition. In contrast to both, English empirical science, under the influence of Bacon, Boyle, and Gassendi, among others, championed experience as a source of knowledge, albeit with a more limited understanding of truth than that sought by Aristotelians or Cartesians. Locke, with his claim to experience, cut a defining figure in "the development of a family of ideas that breached the epistemological barrier between a logic and rhetoric, or knowledge and opinion."[17]

This is not to say that either rhetorical or philosophical notions and practices remained unchanged by this breach. On the contrary, these new empirical scientists reworked established modes of authorizing claims to assert and legitimate their innovations in philosophy and science.[18] The new emphasis on experimental natural philosophy challenged Aristotelian and Cartesian philosophy, on the one hand, and the Pyrrhonian skepticism of Montaigne, on the other. These challenges did not necessitate a radical break with these traditions, however. Instead, early empirical scientists drew from a range of traditions that they reworked for their distinctive purposes. The influence of Montaigne and other skeptics is registered in the prominent role of contingency and the persistent threat of fallible senses. Their *mitigated* skepticism, however, focused on modes of judgments based on experience that were registered as more or less probable. Such evidence from experience, judged by a matter of degrees rather than certain truth or falsity, challenged traditions of appealing to authoritative texts favored by both Aristotelians and humanists.[19] With the new notion of probable judgment reworked from the rhetorical tradition, these experimental scientists sought authority for their new claims to knowledge, based not in tradition but in contingent experience.

This project required new methods of evaluation to distinguish matters of fact from the products of unquestioned opinion and fallible senses. In turning to experience as a source of knowledge, the English empirical scientists did not consider all experience to be equal. They developed experimental methods, but not all sources of knowledge could come from direct observation. Testimony and reports of others were also necessary, if not always as reliable. The Royal Society developed new standards and gradations of probability in order to evaluate testimony and determine what could be considered a "matter of fact" under conditions of incomplete or contested information.[20] While truth through demonstration was often out of reach, a range of terms indicating degrees of uncertainty could be applied, among them *highly probable, probable, mere opinion,* and *conjecture.*[21]

It is important to note that probability in this era did not entail the highly formalized mathematical methods used by social scientists today, though it could involve quantification. These early empirical philosophers considered carefully, both qualitatively and quantitatively, when assent to philosophical claims was warranted. They based assent, for example, on the number and reliability of first-hand testimony and secondhand reports whose reliability might be determined by personal characteristics of observers, for example, their skill, education, and personal stakes in the outcome. These emerging scientific methods borrowed heavily from practices for evaluating the reliability of witnesses and their testimony, as established in legal practice and with roots in the rhetorical tradition.[22] Where opinion had previously been excluded from the purview of science, a central question for this new natural philosophy was which opinions could be trusted as evidence of knowledge or were close enough to be useful.[23]

The Royal Society and its adherents were not simply taking up a new mode of scientific inquiry for a narrow group of experts. They sought new modes of reporting probabilistic claims based on experience to audiences for whom such claims were unfamiliar.[24] Reporting of experimental findings was indispensable for this new scientific method and it was also essential for winning approval and support. They needed, in other words, to persuade new audiences of their experimental claims without a claim to philosophical certainty. Consequently, the new articulation of probable knowledge drawn from experience generates more than a new epistemology. To substantiate the conclusions drawn from an experiment and enable others to build upon that knowledge required that witnesses be present and their presence recorded. Experimental reports, Boyle argued, must be written so as to allow others to replicate the experiment without having been present, scrupulously recounting their methods, materials, and circumstances. Such careful performance of experiment and the recording of *direct* observation, however, were insufficient for the aspirations of the Royal Society, which hoped to convey their findings to a much larger public than those who might ever serve as direct observers. They sought to expand their claims of experience through vivid narratives of their experiments so they could create, in Steven Shapin's words, "virtual witnesses."[25] Modes of writing aimed at eliciting the experience of observation, at bringing knowledge back to the senses, came to be essential for the launching of novel scientific claims through a vocabulary of probability, opinion, and experience drawn and reworked from the rhetorical tradition.

Recognizing the intersection of philosophical and rhetorical traditions and the ongoing place of rhetoric in this emerging scientific culture makes a difference for how we understand Locke's claim to experience in the *Essay*. Resituating Locke within the context of early English empirical philosophy troubles the long-standing association of Locke with philosophy against rhetoric and perceptual experience against language. Douglas Casson shows how extensively this new wave of probable judgment informs *An Essay Concerning Human Understanding* and Locke's body of work as a whole, including his writings on religion and politics. The *Essay*, in fact, comes to enact the very shift from demonstrative certainty to probability that Shapiro and others have highlighted historically. In book 4 of the *Essay*, Locke asserts what seems like a hard and fast distinction between knowledge and opinion, reiterating the traditional opposition between *scientia* and *opinio*. He defines knowledge as "nothing but *the perception of the connexion and agreement, or disagreement and repugnancy of any of our Ideas*" (4.1.1). Such knowledge, described as an immediate perception, is certain and treated as a kind of passive reception in which the understanding has no choice but to accept the proposition in question. Belief or opinion, by contrast, is qualitatively distinguished from knowledge. Belief or opinion requires an active practice of judgment of whether assent should be given to a relation of ideas "when their certain Agreement or Disagreement is not perceived but *presumed* to be so." At this point in the text, Locke describes knowledge and judgment as two different faculties (4.14.4). Most propositions arise as a matter of judgment rather than certainty, and as such they are weighed in terms of probability, or likeliness of truth by degrees (4.15.2–3). This distinction recalls both Aristotelian and Cartesian categories and in part accounts for why so many readers have seen Locke as a confident defender of rational certainty or at least a defender of demonstrative knowledge against uncertain belief.[26]

As several of Locke's interpreters have noted, however, his distinction does not hold.[27] Locke immediately undermines his own clear contrast, ultimately shifting to a *quantitative* distinction between forms of belief and opinion that he treats as knowledge. He cites other forms of knowledge, including habitual knowledge based on the memory of perception; sensitive knowledge of the existence of external objects; and demonstrative knowledge, which is mediated by other propositions. Locke assigns the term *knowledge* to all these, but none of them uphold the same immediate and passive reception initially required for knowledge. Consequently, as Casson summarizes these moves, "Locke pushes the greater part of our knowledge in the direction of voluntary belief" and probability effectively takes over the realm of knowledge.[28]

Locke never fully abandons his claims to certain knowledge, notably asserting that "*Morality is capable of Demonstration,* as well as *Mathematicks*" (3.11.16; see also 4.3.18). Indeed, there are for Locke cases in which such assent will be forced by demonstrably true claims, but they turn out to be infrequent and highly limited in practical use. These truths, such as "Where there is no Property, there is no Injustice" remain meaningful only at the level of abstract definition. Locke holds out the promise of demonstrative certainty in moral philosophy but never develops it, and it is unclear whether it could ever be developed.[29] In other words, Locke reserves a category of knowledge that is certain and immediate. Over the course of book 4 of the Essay, however, that category comes to occupy an increasingly circumscribed and irrelevant place in the work's central concern with the conduct of human understanding and action. Belief or opinion based on active judgment of when to give assent takes over most matters before the understanding. The narrow scope of demonstrative knowledge and the vast, expansive terrain of judgment are brought together under the chapter heading "Reason." In this comprehensive form, reason emerges, in William Walker's words as "the faculty that bridges the supposedly distinct faculties of Knowledge and Judgment and that assesses and is affected by all ideas, whether they make up knowledge or probability."[30] Locke resituates reason such that it no longer sits on the side of either philosophy or opinion. Rather, reason is expanded to encompass judgment in situations both certain and uncertain, but mostly uncertain. Despite the lack of certainty, Locke speaks of judgment as sufficient for the purposes that humans face as moral and instrumental agents in this life and the next. Judgment in practical matters is both necessary and sufficient for even the weightiest matters of human action and responsibility. As Kirstie McClure explains, for Locke, "the dilemma confronting every human agent was one not of metaphysical speculation but of existential risk and practical judgment."[31]

Recognizing Locke as a theorist of judgment may seem discordant with his appeals throughout his writings to foundationalist terms and tropes, for example, the grounds of knowledge, philosophical and political origins, and nature as representing both a human condition (the state of nature) and functioning as an object of scientific inquiry. It certainly challenges the construction of his work as fundamentally divided. However, it also challenges those who see a more unified body of work in which practical judgments find their validity by recourse to epistemological or moral foundations, whether empirical, rational, religious or some combination of these.[32] Instead, Locke's appeal to such foundationalist terms sets up a problematic of judgment that does not guarantee verifiable conclusions, at least not in this life. It is this problematic of judgment that, as we will see in the forthcoming chapters, bridges his philosophical, moral, and political concerns.

As we now see, Locke's claim to experience and his overriding concern with judgment emerge from a period of cross-pollination between traditions of rhetoric and of philosophy. While new natural philosophers adopted the older rhetorical language of experience, opinion, and probability, they also reinvented that language for their novel scientific projects. Such reinvention, however, does not necessarily mark the severing of rhetoric's influence on the notion of experience.[33] Rather, the reworking of an old language for new purposes and the desire to disseminate sensible experience and practices of observation to an emerging public made vivid language, analogies from nature, and the capacity to persuade an audience of probable truths all the more important. In other words, the reinvention of a language of experience and a mode of judgment out of fraying philosophical and humanistic traditions relied on rhetoric in new, distinctive ways.

The Culture of Epicurean Materialism

I have so far placed greater emphasis on how the notion of probable judgment drawn from experience borrowed from the rhetorical tradition and was reinvented for the scientific purposes of emerging claims to experience in natural philosophy. This preoccupation with probabilistic judgment was by no means limited to what we would recognize today as an emerging scientific realm. On the contrary, it came to span many types of inquiry that included not only philosophy and science but also history, religion, language, and politics.[34] It became, in Richard Kroll's words, "an entire symbolic cultural mode."[35] This cultural mode was one of Epicurean materialism, inaugurated by Gassendi's revival of Epicurus, via the poetry of Lucretius (translated into English for the first time in 1656), and the reconciliation of the ancient philosophy with Christianity.[36] It cohered around the epistemological commitments we have been examining—probable knowledge based in experience, an ineliminable condition of contingency, a mitigated form of skepticism—as well as a revival of Epicurus's commitments to atomism and hedonism. Emerging in the aftermath of the English civil wars, these widespread commitments and themes contributed to an anti-Cartesian perspective held by Gassendi, as well as Boyle, an important intellectual influence for Locke, and Hobbes, in differing ways.[37] Notably, in contrast to Descartes and Spinoza, Gassendi insisted on the necessity of rhetoric for this new method and epistemology.[38]

Language was a matter of significant interest and concern from the beginning for the New Scientists. Just as Aristotelian and humanist approaches to empirical inquiry fell short, so too did they fail to offer an appropriate language with which conduct the methods and convey the findings of the New Science. Bacon first suggested aphorism and analogy as particularly useful styles, but his model was not adopted by later generations of the Royal Society. By the second half of the seventeenth century, the distrust of Aristotelian and humanist practices were combined with a particularly intense hostility to the unstructured, emotive, and mystical rhetoric of nonconformist sects (enthusiasts) who also rejected their predecessors. A new style for the New Science sought to reject the highly ornate, disputational, and impassioned speech of these various opponents, for purposes of knowledge as well as politics. Nevertheless, rhetoric remained essential for their philosophical and practical purposes.[39]

Language and a renewed interest in the workings of the material world were not necessarily opposed but were brought into close relation in this new materialism, as exemplified in an oft-cited analogy by Lucretius comparing letters with atoms.[40] Where *materialism* today often connotes mechanism, contingency was instead a central commitment for this seventeenth-century materialist culture along with a rhetoric that promoted that sense of contingency. Objects of inquiry, natural, historical, or textual, were approached as fragments or atoms from which to draw hypothetical inferences. Such atoms—whether scriptural fragments or natural evidence—were resistant, but not immune, to interpretation. Their stubbornly fragmented nature served to highlight the artificial and contingent work of drawing meaning from the particulars of experience.[41]

The atomistic nature of the material world pressed the need for the intervention and artifice of the interpreter or judge. Self-conscious activities of interpretation and judgment were seen as essential to moral, historical, scientific, and philosophical knowledge, whether in reading scripture, ancient texts, or the Book of Nature.[42] Accordingly, Epicurean writers engaged in a self-narration of their own reading to "allude to and dramatize the reader's necessarily contingent activity when faced with the text," revealing to readers the conditions of the texts own production, particularly its figural devices.[43] Performing its own creation, especially its rhetorical creation, proceeded, at least in part, through certain conventions that we find in Locke's *Essay*. These include the soliciting of the reader's assent and the implication that such assent will be shared by other readers. In this way, the reader is invited into the activity of interpreting the text by the text itself, emphasizing how meaning is produced in contingent encounters between reader and text. In this way, both the skepticism of Montaigne and the need to move on with cautious judgment are registered in a new method and style.[44] This mitigated skepticism required careful attention to the appropriate conduct with which one might negotiate that contingency when approaching a text or an experiment. It did not aspire, however, to the elimination of that contingency.

Turning back once more to the epistle to the *Essay*, we can draw still richer meaning from these passages by recognizing the way that it participates in the textual practices of Epicurean materialist culture. To recall, Locke presents to his readers a scene, in which "five or six Friends meeting at my Chamber . . . found themselves quickly at a stand, by the Difficulties that rose on every side." The *Essay* thus begins with a narrative of the conditions of its own production. Those conditions are contingent ("by Chance"), social ("five or six Friends"), and materially situated ("at my Chamber") (7). As a precursor to inquiry, Locke recounts an epistemological crisis in which this friendly group must navigate what first appears to be irresolvable doubt. Rather than giving in to radical skepticism, however, they stop and redirect their efforts, turning first inward: "before we set our selves upon Enquiries of that Nature, it was necessary to examine our own abilities, and see, what Objects of our Understandings were, or were not fitted to deal with." The mode of inquiry for this group, as well as for the author of the *Essay*, is self-conscious. Ultimately, the epistle draws readers as well into this self-conscious activity, as Locke asks them to observe in themselves analogous phenomena of the understanding.[45]

The scene evokes both crisis and possibility, clearing the way for a chastened and arduous reconstruction of the fragments of knowledge. The way forward, both cautious and civil, is not the project of a lone philosopher but is a shared venture hinging on mutual assent: "This I proposed to the Company who all readily assented; and thereupon it was agreed, that this should be our first Enquiry." The epistle links this contingent occasion and mode of inquiry to the rhetorical style of the *Essay*. Locke apologetically describes his work as "[s]ome hasty and undigested Thoughts, on a Subject I had never before considered . . . which having been thus begun by Chance, was continued by Intreaty; written by incoherent parcels; and, after long intervals of neglect, resum'd again, as my Humour or occasions permitted." What appears as a claim to no style we now recognize as participating in the plain style of the New Science, as Locke challenges the "*[v]ague and insignificant Forms of Speech and Abuse of Language*" that "have so long passed for Mysteries of Science."

Even more, however, the epistle shows us how the style itself expresses the social and material conditions of the experience of the author and his friends. The writing must stop and start again, like this circle of friends, cognizant of their limitations. Both participants and style proceed in a fragmented and discontinuous manner, subjected to the contingent forces of humor, chance, and entreaty. The epistle draws the reader into the contingent experience of its birth and its voice, apologizing for it but at the same time widening the circle of cooperative inquiry conducted by underlaborers seeking only to "remove some of the Rubbish, that lies in the way to Knowledge." In expanding his circle to an untold number of readers, Locke lends the *Essay* a quality of never being fully realized.

The narrative of the epistle enacts the reconstructive turn to origins that the *Essay* will advance as its primary mode of inquiry and that echoes through the *Two Treatises of Government*. The rhetorical form of the *Essay* is appropriate to the mode of inquiry and the mode of inquiry is enacted in the rhetorical style of the *Essay*. Rhetoric and method drive each other in the shared pursuit of limited claims drawn from contingent, material conditions. Specifically, Locke adopts the genre of the essay, following in the footsteps of both Montaigne and Bacon. In a similar spirit in which Bacon advocated aphorism so that philosophers could convey "'knowledge broken' to invite further inquiry," Locke as essayist advances the informal and winding form of the essay to fit the fragmented and contingent nature of his findings.[46] As Theodor Adorno would observe centuries later: "Discontinuity is essential to the essay; its subject matter is always a conflict brought to a standstill."[47]

As we will see later, this depiction prefigures Locke's exploration of the human understanding in a social scene figured as a "presence-room" and an intimate scene of acquaintance between the understanding and truth.[48] More generally, the epistle launches a manner of conducting the inquiry of the human understanding in a way that vividly depicts Locke's experience of the understanding with an invitation to his readers to join in the inquiry and give their assent, that is, an invitation to exercise their judgment in a chastened, collaborative effort. Such contingency extends forward to the reception of the book as Locke addresses himself to readers of varying temperaments and imaginations, as well as to the possibility of favorable and unfavorable judgments (8–9). For "he that thinks the same Truth shall be equally relished by every one in the same dress, may as well hope to feast every one with the same sort of Cookery" (8). It will, Locke complains, "not be easie to persuade, either those who speak, or those who hear them, that they are but the Covers of Ignorance, and hindrance of true Knowledge" (10). Locke's task in the *Essay* laid out here is to challenge not just established traditions of knowledge but a particular way of speaking about objects of the understanding or ideas, both sensed and artificed. He is concerned, perhaps above all, with the ways that such ideas circulate in society, in the languages of sects and in polite conversation. A care for words, both concern and attention, and their impact on the understanding and on society and politics is at the forefront from the opening pages of the *Essay*.

I do not mean to suggest that all writers in late seventeenth-century England, including Locke, were working with the same notions of knowledge or language by virtue of a cultural influence of Epicurean materialism. Quite to the contrary, disparate understandings of the relationship between knowledge and language abounded (not least of them offered by Locke), each inheriting, contesting, and reworking in distinctive ways the legacies of Aristotelian philosophy, humanism and the rhetorical tradition, and Pyrrhonian skepticism.[49] Instead, I point to the ways that questions of language intersect with the challenge of understanding the material world and the appropriate modes of conduct and judgment for humans in this world and in the next. Such emerging claims of experience relied upon writing and styles of argumentation to authorize new methods and modes of judgment. The aurality of speech and the visuality of writing, for good or bad, could be seen as having a materializing force, a way of rendering experience vivid, in science as well as politics. An opposition between language and matter, in other words, is not inevitable. Rather, language is both reflective and productive of material experience. The culture of Epicurean materialism invites us to think about language as a material and materializing force, essential for the communication of experience to others. Locke's philosophical and political writings are a particularly compelling site in which to do so because of their strong association with one side of these dichotomies as the sole basis for critique. As we will find by examining his *Essay* in this light, claims to experience could require, just as they might be used to contest, the force of rhetoric.

As we have seen, Locke does not spare harsh words for rhetoric as "mere" persuasion, connoting deception at worst and mere ornament at best. Nevertheless, this does not preclude a more productive role for rhetoric that sustains his philosophical project. Further, this is not to reserve for rhetoric solely a role as philosophy's handmaiden but, rather, to recognize how imaginative language is necessary for creating the conditions for rational thought and critique. What it means for reading the *Essay*, and ultimately the *Two Treatises*, is that the abundant metaphors used by writers of the Royal Society are more than ornamental. As Paul de Man reminds us, such figural language carries significance beyond its power to deceive, decorate, or otherwise render palatable the claims of philosophy. Imaginative language, in other words, contributes to the meaning of texts, even those of philosophy, with both creative and disruptive forces.[50] In recognizing the unruliness of Locke's figural language, however, de Man sees in his work only a conflict between philosophy and rhetoric and a challenge to the author's authoritative voice. While de Man understood this capacity of rhetoric to generate meaning in ways without which philosophy cannot proceed, he could not imagine Locke's relation to such figural language in any other way than antagonistic. Grassi shares de Man's dismissal of Locke as an enemy of rhetoric. However, Grassi sets out a model for us of rereading the history of philosophy to locate theoretical resources for understanding rhetoric's constitutive role, orienting us to the rhetorical tradition in particular. We do well to bring to Locke's thought both theorists' insights in searching for rhetoric's creative and disruptive capacities, without their assumptions of his rationalism. In reading Locke's *Essay* more closely, we will be attentive to the ways that rhetoric is productive of meaning and even of philosophical claims, including but not limited to those of method and readerly judgment. In doing so, we will recover the essential place of rhetoric—its figures and invention—in Locke's project of critique.

Rereading the Claim to Experience

Let us turn now to Locke's claim to experience as it unfolds in books 1 and 2 of the *Essay* to see how it draws upon Epicurean materialist rhetorical practices to challenge the philosophical authorities of the day and clear the way for a new modes of establishing the authority of one's judgments. The hallmarks of Epicurean materialist writing are not limited to the epistle and, in fact, the practices that we observed in the epistle return in book 1. As we move into the body of the *Essay*, these practices of style and genre of the epistle take on a more substantive character, with transformative, and unsettling, implications for the meaning of experience as the grounds of judgment.

In book 1, the *Essay* opens with a crisis of doubt in the form of a skeptical attack on innate ideas that serves as a prelude to an alternative, more cautious and limited project of interpretation and judgment.[51] Whereas the epistle recounted how Locke and his friends found themselves at a standstill, in book 1 Locke seeks to generate for his readers a similar impasse with regard to the claims of timeless and universal truths understood as divinely implanted innate ideas. In his doing so, his claim to experience can emerge from the epistemological ruins of skepticism. His challenge raises not just a question of philosophy but also one of authority more generally (1.1.7, 2). For, as he writes in *Of the Conduct of the Understanding*, "[T]he ideas and images in men's minds are the invisible powers that constantly govern them, and to these they all universally pay a ready submission."[52] Innatists, for Locke, claim such governing authority for their ideas and propositions, an authority that they claim continuously across time and space. For Locke, this poses a practical as well as a philosophical problem for individuals and society.

Locke counters the universality of innatism by asserting, even dramatizing, the plurality of ideas and practices found in the world. In this way, he reinforces the fragmentary nature of human knowledge of the world. The main thrust of his refutation of innate ideas is that knowledge, social practices, and beliefs currently observed or recalled from history and memory show how any idea or practice, no matter how seemingly obvious or necessary, can always be found to be otherwise. He shows how commonly humans depart from allegedly universal, innate ideas, as in the case of "*Children, Ideots, Savages*, and the grosly *Illiterate*" (1.2.27). Among these, Locke returns most often to the figure of the child. Children comprehend only particular ideas, not yet being able to meaningfully form abstract and general ideas. For "[t]he Senses at first let in particular *Ideas*, and furnish the yet empty Cabinet. . . . Afterwards the Mind proceeding farther, abstracts them, and by Degrees learns the use of general Names." As these "Materials" of the mind increase, the mind has more to employ itself with and "the use of Reason becomes daily more visible" (1.2.15).[53] For Locke, children serve as an ordinary example of the particular nature of allegedly innate ideas.

The child is the first scene of Locke's account of the acquisition of ideas through experience, developing over time and across contingent location. In speaking of the formation of a child's understanding, he uses the image of an empty cabinet that becomes furnished initially only with particular ideas drawn from a child's limited range of sensory perceptions, such as colors and tastes (1.1.15, 1.2.25). The limited and common nature of these particular ideas explains how seemingly everyone can share the same basic ideas even if they come from experience rather than God. Those basic ideas, for example, the taste of sweet and bitter, are not timeless truths, but instead quite constrained by contingent situation. The force of the material world writes on the child's understanding, which like white paper "receives any Characters" (2.3.22). Where innatists speak of the mind as imprinted by God, Locke repurposes this metaphor such that the printing of characters is effected by experience on an ongoing basis.[54] It is the material character of writing that Locke uses to resignify the nature of ideas. Thinking about ideas from the perspective of the child disrupts the unbounded continuity of innatism while at the same time resituating ideas on the finite and particular terrain of a changing human mind and body.

The child is also important in a very different set of examples, more threatening than ordinary. Locke vividly dramatizes the unbounded diversity of human convention and belief by pointing to the frequency with which moral rules are violated and ideas of God may not be found at all (1.4.9, 14). Robbery, murder, and rape are cited as widespread examples of the absence of moral agreement. He departs from such ordinary violations in a series of foreign examples of "savage" practices drawn from travel literature.[55] Locke recites conventions of burying children alive among the Mengrelians and of gelding children among the Caribes, and he writes of Garcilaso de la Vega's Peruvians, who are "wont to fat and eat the Children they got on their female Captives, whom they kept as Concubines for that purpose; and when they were past Breeding the Mothers themselves were kill'd too and eaten" (2.3.9). Locke lists a fair number of these cases, which are also notable for the way that they seem to deny the principle that Locke identifies as a natural duty in the *Two Treatises*: that of parents to provide for their children. What is boundless, on Locke's account, is not truth of which we can be certain but, rather, the plurality of cultural practices that display instead a striking violation of anything one might assume to be universal or natural.

With his tales of cannibals and focus on the child, Locke in book 1 of the *Essay* is at his closest to the skepticism of Montaigne's *Essais*, especially in Montaigne's essay "Of Cannibals."[56] Like Montaigne, Locke seeks to defamiliarize the customary in order to chasten unbounded claims to knowledge and authority. His tales of cannibals and godlessness do not simply seek to instill a fear of the unfamiliar, though that may be one effect; no less significant, these examples help to generate a critical perspective on familiar practices. By the end of book 1, there is little left to suggest any necessary or fixed order to human life, even in matters pertaining to religion. The unsettling practices cited by Locke redraw the territory of knowledge, such that claims to truth and morality must be recognized as bounded and partial.

The critique of innate ideas clears the deck of some of Locke's opposition, but that is not all it does. Locke's tales of godlessness, cannibalism, and infanticide, in the New World as well as the Old, stages a significant disruption. For many of his contemporaries, the rejection of innate ideas and propositions was disturbing to religion and morality, and the *Essay* was "deemed by not a few to be dangerous" in its influence at Oxford and Cambridge.[57] Locke generates dissonance in ways of speaking and understanding the world in terms of continuity and repetition over time and space. This dissonance is generated both from Montaignean questioning and from his more credulous claim of experience. He insinuates this disruption with the very image of imprinted ideas used by innatists, which he resituates within contingent human perception and practices. Humans become the authors of their ideas, but not without risk. Imprinted by experience, the human understanding in Locke's treatment is capable of unlimited diversity, but not unlimited knowledge.

Locke's disruption is made through what we can recognize as two kinds of appeals to experience. First, he advances his skeptical critique of innatism by reference to the particular, to the social practices of diverse communities. He shows in dramatic form that human knowledge is limited and beliefs and practices are conditioned by social context. In this way, he calls upon experience as shared practices to serve as counterevidence to the universalism based in an otherworldly order. Such shared experience is anything but universal. Instead of merely denying the fact of innate ideas, he vividly brings to the fore the diversity of moral, political, and legal practices—what we might also call the diversity of claims of authority. Such evidence depends, of course, on the testimony of others, specifically travel writers. Locke adapts the rhetorical conventions of the reports of travel writers, for whom "reports of barbarism and savagery were a stock in trade," to advance his attack on innate ideas.[58] The other claim of experience proceeds from the individuated experience of the human understanding, represented in the ordinary examples of the child, which is not so obviously disruptive. Rather, with the ordinary example of the child, we are reminded of the change and partiality of each individual understanding, that is, the contingent and limited nature of knowledge based in experience. As we will see in the following section, this ordinary case of the understanding in progress posits a discontinuity in the human understanding itself that may be even more unsettling than the reports of cannibalism and infanticide.

The Lockean Subject: Disruptive and Disrupted

The portrait of the child's gradual accumulation of ideas—constrained by time and place—bridges books 1 and 2. Through it, experience becomes an origin of knowledge that is an alternative to innate ideas: "He that attentively considers the state of a *Child*, at his first coming into the World, will have little reason to think him stored with plenty of *Ideas*, that are to be the matter of his future Knowledge.

'Tis by degrees he comes to be furnished with them." Locke sets his subject in motion here, a self changing over time, in response to encounters with the world. That world is, in the first place, a material world: "But all that are born in to the World being surrounded with Bodies, that perpetually and diversely affect them, variety of *Ideas*, whether care be taken about it or no, are imprinted on the Minds of children. *Light*, and *Colours*, are busie at hand every where, when the Eye is but open; *Sounds*, and some *tangible Qualities* fail not to solicite their proper Senses, and force an entrance to the Mind" (2.1.6).[59] Experience in this sense is identified with two "Fountains of Knowledge," both types of perception (2.1.2). The first, as we see in the passage above, is an external perception, that is, of sight, sound, taste, and so on. The second is internal, a perception of the activities of one's own understanding, for example, sensing, thinking, doubting, believing, imagining, reasoning (2.1.3–4). Internal perception is a self-reflexive activity that enables one to reflect on the understanding as thinking self as well as on those ideas furnished from without. Even with seemingly purely physical sensations such as pain, perceptions are understood by Locke to involve the entry of an idea of pain into the understanding. Perception is an internal event even when ideas are set in motion by external bodies.

It is easy to interpret this strange account of ideas as a radical separation of mind and body, whereby even pain and pleasure must be perceived as intellectual events, rather than unmediated bodily occurrences. At his most extreme, Locke claims that without *ideas* of sensations in the understanding, "there is no Perception. Fire may burn our Bodies, with no other effect, than it does a Billet, unless the motion be continued to the Brain, and there the sence of Heat, or *Idea* of Pain, be produced in the Mind, wherein consists *actual Perception*" (2.9.3). This claim must be tempered, however, with his other example of the fairly ordinary example of a person tuning out sound as well as his claim that "[a] Man on the Rack, is not at *liberty* to lay by the *Idea* of pain, and divert himself with other Contemplations" (2.21.12). The image of a burning body with no idea, and thus no perception, of pain appears as a most striking case of a "veil of ideas," but it hyperbolically demonstrates a different point. Locke emphasizes here that perception *must* involve both idea and sensation, a stimulation of both body and mind. As these examples suggest, Locke invokes the language of mind-body dualism, but it is undercut by his insistence on the joint role of mind and body as constitutive of perception. The body does not experience pain apart from the understanding just as the understanding does not think without embodied perception. Nicholas Jolley calls Locke's stance that of a "weak" materialist, one that is far more agnostic on metaphysical issues than either the materialism of Hobbes or the rational-ism of Descartes.[60]

According to Locke, ideas of perception arrive in the understanding in atomis-tic form, that is, as simple ideas from sense or reflection, unmixed with other perceptions. They furnish the storehouse of the understanding and become acces-sible through memory (2.2.1–2). These ideas stored in memory in turn become material for the activities of the understanding, such as combining and separating ideas into complex and abstract ideas. Sometimes the original imprinting of such ideas can be recalled, though it also begins before the understanding can register such experience as memory (2.1.6). Locke expresses confidence in our knowledge of such uncompounded perceptions, more so than with any more complex ideas. As situations call for more complex ideas, there is greater room for confusion and presumption. While simple ideas may be understood as building blocks, they are not necessarily the starting point for reconstruction of a worldly or universal order with any certainty. In an Epicurean materialist frame, such atoms can be seen as fragments of a whole that can be reconstructed (if at all) only up to a point and always with remaining uncertainty. Locke's simple ideas serve as material for the cautious (re-)creation of relations out of fragments, analogous to the piecing together and interpretation of an ancient text.[61]

Locke's faith in simple ideas must be read in the context of a more complicated relationship between the material world and the human understanding. One of the most familiar representations of the Lockean mind is as a passive receptor for sense perceptions, a mirror held up to the observable world.[62] Locke uses this language of passive reception at times, but it should be understood as one among several modes of perception and mental states. He speaks of the activity of paying attention as another means of acquiring ideas through sensation. Even more trou-bling for this traditional account, the understanding's passive receptivity does not always produce the calm and mastery also traditionally associated with the Lock-ean mind. Sensory experience easily intrudes on a passive understanding, not always waiting for its attention or interest. "*Light,* and *Colours,* are busie at hand every where, when the Eye is but open; *Sounds,* and some *tangible Qualities* fail not to *solicite* their proper Senses, and force an entrance to the Mind" (2.1.6). Sensa-tion can be an unsolicited force. Unlike the gentle author of the epistle, they do not always wait for assent.

Unsolicited sensations are just one way that the understanding is subject to forced entry. The passivity of sensation is linked as well to passions associated with particular ideas and memories, even simple sensory ideas. In fact, "there is scarce any affection of our Senses from without, any retired thought of our Mind within, which is not able to produce in us *pleasure* or *pain*" (2.7.2). Most ideas—simple or complex, sensory or reflective—are felt passionately, either positively or negatively. Without such affective charge, neither our minds nor bodies would be spurred to action, leaving one "a very idle unactive Creature" (2.7.3). Ideas of pleasure and pain are important for motivating action as well as self-preservation as they register microlevel, barely detectable judgments of what is helpful and harmful in perception and memory.[63] In this way, Locke writes, in a manner characteristic of his century, of passions as both troubling and necessary.[64]

Pain and pleasure are themselves simple ideas for Locke, but they are distinctive in that they frequently accompany other ideas, making a special connection to action as well as memory.[65] They operate on both mind and body, as in the case of blushing caused by shame (2.20.17). They sometimes threaten to carry the understanding away from a course of its own choosing, with a force more powerful than sense perceptions alone: "sometimes a boisterous Passion hurries our Thoughts, as a hurricane does our Bodies, without leaving us the liberty of thinking on other things, which we would rather chuse" (2.21.12). Locke presents the understanding as rendered passive by sensation and by passions as ordinary, a condition that is both necessary and potentially problematic. While sensory and passionate experience prove indispensable to the understanding, it can hinder more complex and abstract thoughts when the understanding becomes incapable of directing its attention.

Memory, like perception, encompasses active and passive states. The understanding can revive an idea formerly perceived but now hidden, to "paint them anew on it self" (2.10.2). This capacity for recollection, along with perception, is the condition of all other capacities of the understanding (2.10.8). Even the ordinary workings of memory are inevitably prone to loss, however: "*Ideas* in the Mind quickly fade, and often vanish quite out of the Understanding, leaving no more footsteps or remaining Characters of themselves, than Shadows do over Fields of Corn; and the Mind is as void of them, as if they never had been there" (2.10.4).[66] Those "characters," once imprinted by experience on the understanding, are prone to change and erasure. Locke's discussion of memory takes a melancholy turn as he links the mortality of our bodies and of our minds: "Thus the *Ideas*, as well as Children, of our Youth, often die before us: And our Minds represent to us those Tombs, to which we are approaching; where though the Brass and Marble remain, yet the Inscriptions are effaced by time, and the Imagery moulders away. *The Pictures drawn in our Minds, are laid in fading Colours; and if not some-*

times refreshed, vanish and disappear" (2.10.5). This image of memory highlights the shifting nature of the understanding's storehouse, like our fluctuating and declining physical state as mortals. The instability of memory is intensified by the fact that memories do not always wait to be recalled but "start up in our Minds of their own accord, and offer themselves to the Understanding; and very often are rouzed and tumbled out of their dark Cells, into open Day-light, by some turbulent and tempestuous Passion; our Affections bringing *Ideas* to our Memory, which had otherwise lain quiet and unregarded" (2.10.7). The understanding is rendered passive by the force of decay and of unexpected, intruding memories, especially those involving passions.

As we are beginning to see, Locke's account of the entry of perceptions as simple ideas is more complex than it appears initially. Passions, themselves simple ideas, come attached to ideas of all kinds, including simple sensory perceptions (2.7.3–4). Such attachments serve important functions as motivation and warning, but they also suggest that simple ideas come into our perception with complications and attachments. As Locke acknowledges, "the Qualities that affect our Senses, are, in the things themselves, so united and blended, that there is no separation, no distance between them." Such a recognition does not deter him from his belief in simple ideas, however: "yet 'tis plain, the *Ideas* they produce in the Mind, enter by the Senses simple and unmixed" (2.2.1).

What is interesting about this tension is less that we may be catching Locke in a logical misstep, but rather that he openly invites his readers to recognize experience as simple and fragmented, on the one hand, and prone to unchosen attachment and relation, on the other. It is characteristic of Locke's discontinuous style in the *Essay* that he lays out for display the sometimes confounding possibilities afforded by experience, including his own experience of the understanding. The result is a portrait of the human understanding situated in contingent experience that is sensory and reflective, recollected and passionate. It is an embodied subject, dependent on sensory perception, that is prone to flux. Locke's understanding of a self is constituted out of this fluctuating entry and exit of ideas into the "presence-room" of the understanding. This is not to say that such change and disruption is the goal or desired outcome of Locke's *Essay*. It is simply to call attention to the way that Locke's disruption of the timeless universalism of innatists extends to the workings of the human understanding: Locke's disrupted subject follows from his critique of philosophical authority. Locke claims experience to refute innatism, but claiming experience brings into sight an unruliness and partiality embedded within his subject.

Association and the Problem of Experience

Nowhere is Locke's concern about the disruptive effects of experience more dramatically displayed than in the last chapter of book 2, where he takes up the "disease" of association. "Association" is the name that Locke gives to the "strong Combination of *Ideas*, not ally'd by Nature, the Mind makes in it self either voluntarily, or by chance, and hence it comes in different Men to be very different, according to their different Inclinations, Educations, Interests, *etc.*," (2.33.6). Such combinations are settled by habit into patterns of thinking: "*Ideas* that in themselves are not at all of kin, come to be so united in some Mens Minds, that 'tis very hard to separate them, they always keep in company, and the one no sooner at any time comes into the Understanding but its Associate appears with it; and if they are more than two which are thus united, the whole gang always inseparable shew themselves together" (2.33.5). For Locke, associations are conventional "Sympathies and Antipathies" that "produce as regular Effects as if they were Natural" (2.33.7). His examples range from the innocuous case of a man who cannot separate his feelings of disgust from the taste of honey to the tragic figure of a mother whose mourning for a lost child is endless to the comic case of a gentleman who is unable to dance without a certain trunk being present in the room (2.33.7–17). In contrast to the case of later empiricists who identify association with reason, for Locke it is an everyday form of "Unreasonableness" (2.33.3). It is a form of madness, but "there is scarce a Man so free from it" (2.33.4).[67] This form of madness is a social as well as an individual phenomenon, as association is to blame for "the Irreconcilable opposition between different Sects of Philosophy and Religion" (2.33.18). Association is a difference in degree rather than in kind from the ordinary operations of the understanding. It is a disease of politics and philosophy as well as of individuals.

At issue in this strange behavior for Locke is the stubborn persistence of combinations of ideas where distinct, simple ideas should be perceived. The understanding projects the effects of its own operations onto the world, perceiving particular relations as necessary rather than contingent.[68] It requires the capacity of imagination to "joyne several ideas together which we never observed to exist together."[69] Association reveals the powerful cognitive forces at play in the Lockean understanding, especially imagination as a source of individual difference and unpredictability. The difference between sufferers of association and those unafflicted by the disease is one of degree rather than kind.[70] Those suffering from the madness of association combine ideas using imagination, just as rational thinkers do, but they do so strangely, excessively, and persistently.

What constitutes the excess of association? Locke calls associations unnatural combinations and wrong connections, but they are prompted by encounters in the world. If the dancer had not seen a trunk in the room as he learned to dance, no association between trunk and dancing would have emerged. If experience is the source of knowledge, might it not be sensible to avoid honey if it once made us sick or avoid the doctor who caused us pain? Are we really meant to question the grief of a mourning mother? These relations are experienced together, at least at one point, but for Locke they should not be *necessarily* linked. What is experienced at least once in relation comes to be a powerful attachment and ultimately a habit of the mind and often the body as well. Synonymous with sympathies and antipathies, associations involve intense ideas of pain and pleasure. Painful memories, especially those tied to sickness and death as well as fear, lead to aversions to particular conditions bundled up with those affective memories. Association captures the sense of the passions as both volatile and rendering one passive.[71] Moreover, association shows how bundles of ideas, not just simple ones, enter the understanding by force, repeatedly over time, with unruly effects. Imaginations and passions, through repetition made into habit, acquire such force that associations seem necessary, even universal. Finding universals in perceptual experience for innatists reflects divine work, but for Locke it is human artifice. Recognizing such conventional origins, however, does not dispel the power to bind our judgment and will. Habit is a powerful force. Most troubling for Locke is how such urgently felt relations hold authority over one's own conduct and generate claims on others.

As we now see, experience as the source of knowledge can be quite unruly. Association dramatizes this, but less dramatic versions are even more common: the presence-room of the understanding may find itself populated with unanticipated guests in the form of sensation, and calls to memory may be met with silence. A passive understanding may be open not simply to unmediated sensory encounter of the world but also to small, undetected (pre)judgments about what is desirable or not, threatening or not. The disruptive force of experience in perception, passions, and memory belies the universalism of Aristotelians and Cartesians, destabilizing a powerful mode of authority.[72] Repeating the attachments forged in memory and passions such that they become ingrained habit, however, carries sufficient force to make the understanding perceive the contingent as necessary. In other words, false universals can be drawn from an experiential basis no less than from a belief in innate ideas, particularly when judgments proceed without reflection and are taken as necessary. The claim to experience functions as both disease and cure for Locke. For this reason, it is not enough to simply reject innate ideas, or any similar doctrine. Locke's claim of experience requires that subjects relate to their own habits of mind and body in new ways. If experience is the source of knowledge, how does such a new relation to self and world get off the ground?

$$3$$

MATERIAL WORDS AND SENSIBLE JUDGMENT

Locke's account of experience now comes into focus as far more complex than traditionally recognized. Drawing on a notion of experience that is ultimately inherited from the rhetorical tradition, but reworked for the New Science and a new philosophy, Lockean experience encompasses sensation and passions, imagination and language. As such, it poses a challenge to traditionally authoritative claims to truth. While this multidimensional notion of experience disrupts the timeless universalism of innatists, it creates for Locke a new challenge of reconceiving judgment from the rich, but unruly, grounds of experience. He takes up this challenge, as we will see in this chapter, to offer a model of critical judgment, for the theorist and also for readers. That account of judgment challenges not just an authoritative mode of thinking and reasoning but also a way of speaking that dominates the mind and drives human conduct. Locke thus links experience to language in a new way, rather than seeking to jettison language altogether. His claim to experience depends upon the materializing force of language to bear vivid witness to the human understanding and theorize its critical capacities. Negotiating both the positive and negative effects of material words on humans' understanding and social relations culminates in a judging subject that is marked by anxiety. I argue, however, that such anxious tension is the condition of Lockean critique, whatever uneasiness it may entail.

In the first section of this chapter, we will examine Locke's efforts to limit the unruly effects of passions and imagination through a model of judgment that operates without certain knowledge of a divine or natural order. In the second section, rhetorical figure proves essential to Locke's use of experience as the basis of judgment because it allows the understanding to generate ideas of moral, political, and natural order that exceed the human senses. Alongside Locke's famous castigations of the power of eloquence and misleading nature of metaphor, he appropriates key rhetorical elements for his account of judgment based in experience. Indeed, it is because of the power of rhetoric to influence passionate subjects that he both needs and fears its capacities. We then explore how figure and trope, which sustain Lockean ideas, also underwrite his materialist account of language. Ordinary language is materialist both in the sense that it is based in perceptual experience and in the sense that it plays on the human senses and passions. "Sensible words" highlight Locke's debt to rhetoric because they both draw from and, in turn, generate sensory experience. In the final section, we consider how this debt to rhetoric generates tensions that Locke does not fully resolve. While this unresolved anxiety in Locke's thought can be seen as a failure, I argue instead that it is a necessary feature of Locke's theory and practice of critique. Locke's material words will be indispensable for launching new ways of thinking and speaking that critically engage philosophical, social, and political authority.

Locke's Problematic of Judgment

Perception and memory are the sources of experience out of which the Lockean understanding is constituted and constitutes itself, both actively and passively. The entry and exit of ideas—including the excesses and losses of passions, memory and imagination—constitutes consciousness, which for Locke is the locus of personal identity (2.1.11, 19, 2.27.9). More precisely, it is the perception and memory of the sensations and actions of the body and mind over time from which a self emerges.[1] In this way, the understanding refers to the mind, but also to a broader sense of the self as a totality of shifting but also sedimenting mental, corporeal, and passionate states.

The activities of the understanding are not continuous but often disrupted: by sleep, forgetfulness, and inattention. Yet such disruptions do not preclude the formation of identity across time. Rooted in the recollection of being the same perceiver of actions and sensations of one's own understanding over time,[2] Locke's notion of the self is grounded in a concern for one's past and present actions: "All which is founded in a concern for Happiness the unavoidable concomitant of consciousness, that which is conscious of Pleasure and Pain, desiring, that that *self*, that is conscious should be happy" (2.27.26). The understanding is constituted through contingent situation as well as through the vagaries of passions and memory. Passion and memory, in other words, are conditions of the subject's distinctive identity and a source of instability.

Despite Locke's recognition of the unruliness of the passions, they remain central to his account of the understanding and, in particular, the will: "What moves the mind, in every particular instance, to determine its general power of directing, to this or that particular Motion or rest? And to this I answer, The motive, for continuing in the same State or Action, is only the present satisfaction in it; The motive to change, is always some *uneasiness*" (2.21.29). The greatest and most pressing uneasiness in the mind—a feeling overlapping with, but not identical to, desire—spurs the subject to choices and actions. Generally, pain from an absent good that registers in the understanding as the most pressing uneasiness motivates action. The force of ideas in the understanding, especially passions like pain and pleasure, composes Locke's account of the will. There is no independent or alternative faculty charged with the task of controlling the unruliness associated with perceptions, passions, and memory.[3] This hedonistic account of the will poses a significant challenge because it explains how passionate experience forms the will, but not necessarily in the direction of the greater good. In this respect, Locke faces the challenges of Epicurean materialists more generally in breaking the perception that materialism in general, and hedonism in particular, implies atheism. Yet Locke knew that the rewards and punishments of an afterlife do not necessarily accord with the more pressing desires and pains of personal experience, the experience of embodied creatures in a material world. In this way, Locke's claim to experience generates a problem of judgment.

The disjuncture between Locke's claim to experience involving perception, memory, and passions, on the one hand, and a larger moral order, on the other, is the problematic of judgment to which Locke's philosophical and political writings are addressed.[4] It is a challenge that situates Locke alongside other Epicurean materialists who sought to reconcile passionate and embodied subjects with a Christian worldview.[5] Locke stresses the notion of the greatest good, even as it seems to be undercut by the force of pleasure and pain, that is, uneasiness, to direct the understanding: "[T]he highest perfection of intellectual nature, lies in a careful and constant pursuit of truth and solid happiness; so the care of our selves, that we mistake not imaginary for real happiness, is the necessary foundation for our *liberty*. The stronger ties, we have, to an unalterable pursuit of happiness in general, which is our greatest good, and which as such our desires always follow, the more are we free from any necessary determination of our *will* to any particular action, and from a necessary compliance without desire, set upon any particular" (2.21.51). Humans, Locke insists, are embodied and passionate creatures capable not only of judging the immediate good, but also of fulfilling moral and legal duties in service of the greater good. In fact, the strength of one's attachment to the greater good is essential to moderating the pull of particular desires.

Such self-direction, however, is never guaranteed: "if any extreme disturbance (as sometimes happens) possess our whole Mind, as when the pain of the Rack, an impetuous *uneasiness*, as of Love, Anger, or any other violent Passion, running away with us, allows us not the liberty of thought," there is little human fortitude can accomplish. Yet, under more ordinary conditions, it is possible to direct one's appetites, to "take pains to suit the relish of our Minds to the true intrinsick good or ill, that is in things; and not permit an allow'd or supposed possible great and weighty good to slip out of our thoughts, without leaving any relish, any desire of it still there, till, by a due consideration of its true worth, we have formed appetites in our Minds suitable to it, and made our selves uneasie in the want of it, or in the fear of losing it" (2.21.53). Locke distinguishes between those forms of uneasiness over which we have little control, such as pain inflicted on the body or disease, and other desires of an absent good that "bear proportion to, and depend on the judgment we make" (2.21.57), though, as we have seen, at times, associations and violent passions can acquire the same force. Uneasiness emerges as a result of judgments over time (i.e., habits) and in such cases, humans are accountable for them. Evidence for this is found in the great variety of desires, the ways that different people find relish in different things, as well as the ease with which they are suspended and examined. The understanding, for Locke, has its palate, and it can be cultivated. So too can temporary suspension of action and judgment become a habit. In this way, Locke seeks to marry judgment with desire, even as he recognizes that the understanding will never fully master its own motivating forces.

The challenge of cultivating judgment from the vicissitudes of embodied and passionate creatures is not Locke's alone. As Susan James shows, many seventeenth-century thinkers devised various strategies to respond to the force of the passions. These responses included the notion of dispassionate *scientia*, or certain knowledge, articulated by Descartes and Spinoza, among others.[6] For a diverse group of other thinkers, including Hobbes and the Cambridge Platonists, this notion of scientia lacked the force to move humans to deeper understanding, either scientific or religious. Persuasion was seen as necessary to engaging and redirecting the passions for the sustained inquiry beyond sensible ideas to the intelligible ideas of scientia and for acquiring the appropriate emotional state toward God and the afterlife. Rhetoric moves the passions through vivid images and ingenious similarities where formless, abstract ideas and distant notions of the good cannot. The power of symbols and figural language was an essential means by which to make that which is absent feel present, and the distant and ineffable, accessible. Echoing the rhetorical tradition, thinkers of various stripes recognized the importance of figural and poetic language to negotiate a field of imagination in making moral and rational claims to passionate creatures.[7]

To recognize the necessary force of rhetoric in matters of reason and of faith does not determine the specific role rhetoric may play in relation to truth and reason. Understood instrumentally as "mere" persuasion, rhetoric is limited to the secondary role of helpmate to and ornament of reason. For James, such a secondary role for rhetoric is attributed to many proponents of the New Science, including Hobbes.[8] By contrast, the communication and redirection of passions through figural and poetic language played a primary role in the acquisition of knowledge for Cambridge Platonists and English Puritans, among others.[9]

From among these various responses, Locke is most readily associated with those pursuing new modes of scientia, certainly because of his participation in the Royal Society, but no less for his critiques of innatists as well religious enthusiasts whom he sees as mistaking their passions for the voice of God. Moreover, Locke's insistence that "The last resort a man has recourse to in the conduct of himself is his understanding" suggests a certain wariness toward clergy and other authorities who might stand in as arbiters of truth and for whom rhetoric was long recognized as an integral tool of the trade.[10] So Locke seems naturally affiliated with those most suspicious of rhetoric. His relationship to both scientia and rhetoric, however, is more nuanced than a singular focus on his attacks on rhetoric, imagination, and enthusiasm suggest. As we will see, the judgment required for both moral and scientific thinking in the *Essay* depends on rhetoric in a manner that serves neither solely as helpmate nor to the exclusion of reason.

Locke's response to the problem of judgment and the passions is distinctive from the responses outlined above because he maintains a commitment to reasonable judgment conducted in the absence of certain knowledge of the natural and moral order. Yet he does not abandon sensory and passionate experience as the grounds of judgment. Broadly speaking, for Locke, as for Montaigne, skepticism is an invitation to judgment rather than a foreclosure of it. But for Locke, that judgment is required for acting in both private and public life.[11] The question then becomes how such creatures, constituted through passionate and sensory experience, limited in the compass of their understanding, generate a critical vantage point from which to judge claims of truth and authority as well as one's own actions, desires, and perceptions.

Where passions can be unruly and inconstant, the highest good should be a stable target. Yet this pursuit of a higher good too is driven by a form of attachment, a "stronger tie" or relish. As James Tully explains, Locke's discussion of habit marks a rejection of the Renaissance emphasis on memorization, in favor of physical and mental behavior repeated until it proves pleasurable. Only counterpassions can stand up to the "tyranny" of the passions.[12] It is not, then, a function of a higher-order intellect that masters the passions but one of cultivating particular desires and uneasiness as well as the capacity for suspending action while weighing probabilities of future happiness and pain. How does such judgment get off the ground amid the constant demands of the sensible world? How can human judgment come to give proper weight to more distant and ineffable futures?

Locke does not advocate a retreat from the sensible world, though he believes that humans must cultivate a broader view than what is immediately before them. The challenge is to render the ineffable sensible in order to passionately engage the human understanding. As Tully explains, for Locke, "relish is the mechanism that brings absent goods within one's view of happiness, renders them desirable, and thus disposes the agent to them."[13] Yet this account does not tell us how cultivating such mental relish, that is, the capacity to judge well, gets off the ground. It calls for materializing ideas to give them force for embodied, passionate creatures. Rhetoric carries this materializing force of language to make ideas sensible, that is, to elicit desire and fear in relation to divine authority and the afterlife. But how does Locke tap into this force in light of his misgivings about rhetoric's capacity to mislead judgment? While he may reject the authority of traditional texts associated with the rhetorical tradition and casts aspersions on eloquence, he borrows and repurposes key elements of rhetoric for his account of judgment grounded in experience.

Educating Judgment

Locke offers his most sustained examination of these questions of cultivating judgment from unruly experience and passions, not in the *Essay*, but in *Some Thoughts Concerning Education*. Locke's manual for educating young gentlemen seeks a course for inculcating virtue in passionate, but not yet fully reasonable beings. The end goal of judgment is virtue, which requires a proper relation between reason and appetite: "And the great principle and foundation of all virtue and worth is placed in this, that a man is able to *deny himself* his own desires, cross his own inclinations, and purely follow what reason directs as best though the appetite lean the other way" (*STCE*, §33). This is not a rationality won through the elimination of appetites, however, as "the difference lies not in the having or not having appetites, but in the power to govern and deny ourselves in them" (§36). Neither reason nor virtue can be instilled independently of passions. As in the *Essay*, the basis for good judgment rests in the habit of suspending one's immediate desires to pursue more important goods. In Locke's education, this means learning through habit, of both body and mind, to "relish" esteem and fear disgrace (§§45, 56).[14]

This love of reputation is sufficiently strong to keep a child's other desires in check, for if one can "shame them out of their faults . . . and make them in love with the pleasure of being well thought on, you may turn them as you please, and they will be in love with all the ways of virtue" (§58). This moderation of some passions in favor of others drives many of Locke's recommendations for education, the strange as well as the (now) familiar. Children must be habituated to suspending their desire for physical comfort, for example, by being accustomed to mild discomfort. So Locke recommends that the child's feet "*be washed* every day in cold water, and to have his *shoes* so thin that they might leak and *let in water* whenever he comes near it" (§7). More compassionately, he repeatedly advises restraint in corporal punishment as a counterproductive technique that turns the authority figure (parent or tutor) into an inappropriate model, "lest passion mingle with it [the whipping] and so . . . lose of its due weight: for even children discern when we do things in passion" (§83). Uncontrolled passions unleashed physically or even verbally exert a force on the child's understanding that drives out the attention and emotional states needed for learning: "Passionate words or blows from the tutor fill the child's mind with terror and affrightment, which immediately takes it wholly up and leaves no room for other impressions" (§167).

Hasty punishment risks setting a bad example and carries consequences that are worse than the child's transgression.

In cultivating the right passions in young gentlemen, Locke understands example to be among the most effective pedagogical tools: "But of all the ways whereby children are to be instructed and their manners formed, the plainest, easiest, and most efficacious is to set before their eyes the *examples* of those things you would have them do or avoid. Which, when they are pointed out to them in the practice of persons within their knowledge with some reflection on their beauty or unbecomingness, are of more force to draw or deter their imitation than any discourses which can be made to them" (§82). Rules and instructions, be they handbooks of rhetoric or discourses on morality, give way to practice and imitation (§§184, 188). Children should acquire virtuous models from stories of the Bible and *The Fables of Aesop*, all the better if there are pictures (§§156, 158–9, 189).[15] In other words, Locke rejects systems and rule books for children, in favor of accessible exemplary stories and images. The use of stories and fables is not reserved only for the very young, "but to be continued even as long as they shall be under another's tuition or conduct . . . nothing sinking so gently and so deep into men's minds as *example*" (§82). In acquiring abstract conceptions of virtue, children and adults alike do well to have a particular, material instance, an example available to the senses.

Parents, especially fathers, come to be crucial exemplars themselves (§68). Locke orients parents toward a future, in which children will make judgments of their own, carrying the promise of friendship and the risk of harsh rebuke: "If you would have him stand in awe of you, imprint it *in his infancy*, and as he approaches more to a man admit him nearer to your familiarity; so shall you have him your obedient subject (as is fit) whilst he is a child, and your affectionate friend when he is a man. . . . [I]mperiousness and severity is but an ill way of treating men, who have reason of their own to guide them, unless you have a mind to make your children, when grown up, weary of you and secretly to say within themselves, *when will you die, Father?*" (§40). Parental example comes back to reward or haunt them, accordingly. Locke sees in the child the adult that the child will become and advises parents to provide an education that is affective as well as learned.

This signals an egalitarian dimension of the goals of Locke's education:[16] "We must look upon our children, when grown up, to be like ourselves: with the same passions, the same desires. We would be thought rational creatures, and have our freedom; we love not to be uneasy under constant rebukes and browbeatings" (§41). In this way, Locke's education carries implications that stretch beyond childhood. As he argues, "Children (nay, and men too) do most by example. We are all a sort of chameleons that still take a tincture from things near us; nor is it to be wondered at in children, who better understand what they see than what they hear" (§67). Educating children in the manner Locke prescribes speaks of human nature more generally: the need for countering passions with passions, cultivated through mental and physical habit, and the importance of vivid examples of practical activity presented in a fabular style.[17]

As we have seen with the New Science, so with Locke's new education: traditional modes of style and figure no longer suffice, but vivid forms of writing and speaking are as important as ever. While handbooks of rhetoric, with their rules, figures, and ornamental eloquence are denigrated by Locke, we find that Cicero, Chillingworth, and other writers in the classical and humanist traditions of rhetoric remain among Locke's most elevated examples for the important skill of speaking and writing well (§§185–89).[18] By directing pupils to the original texts themselves, Locke advocates a direct experience with well-crafted language for learning by example. Here in his *Education*, where the careful training of the passions is most at issue—and thus rhetoric its most potentially threatening—exemplars carrying material and rhetorical force are essential to lessons in good judgment, whether in speaking, writing, or acting virtuously.

Rhetoric and the Framework of Judgment

The cultivation of judgment from the terrain of passions and experience in the *Education* presumes a community into which children are born and in which they are raised, a community that includes parents, tutors, and a larger reputational context that work to reinforce right actions and attitudes. In turn, Locke's education aims at an ideal of virtuous, reasonable, and affectionate conversation between the grown son and his father, such that the education reproduces the kind of ethos required to get it off the ground in the first place (§§95–96). As an aspirational model, this tells us much about the centrality of cultivating mental relish as the path to good judgment and virtuous activity. It does not, however, speak to the challenges described by Locke throughout the *Essay* of noisy and wrangling sects, gangs of associationists and enthusiasts, and other unruly subjects for whom passions rule ungoverned. How can those seeking to govern their own understanding, who may not have enjoyed the benefits of Locke's education, work from experience to judge their actions and beliefs reasonably and virtuously? The "conversation" inaugurated between the author of the *Essay* and his reader offers a further context for educating the palate of the mind to relish those more distant, but lasting, goods. Rehearsing the Epicurean materialist convention of revealing the text's conditions of production, Locke discloses the figural dimensions of concepts and language based in experience. As we will see, Lockean judgment in matters of natural and moral philosophy, including ethics, law, and politics, depends on generating a material force for words and concepts that requires rhetoric.

Cultivating reasonable conduct of the understanding depends on the capacity to understand the place of humans within a morally purposive universe. Significant elements of this universe are not immediately discernable by human senses, or are only partially so. Experience, as sensory perception, is indispensable to, but also insufficient for, the understanding's reasonable conduct. Comprehending this universe is simultaneously a question of moral and natural philosophy, both of which require experience and observation as well as rhetorical invention. To see how and why Locke turns to both experience and invention, we must first recognize the limits of perceptual experience for scientific and moral understanding.

The creatures and objects encountered in the material world, what Locke calls "substances," are presented to the understanding only as a bundle of perceptions (2.23.3). What category they belong to—species of plant, animal, or object, for example—is a matter of probable judgment, not a feature of the natural world apparent to human understanding. Even more obscure to the human senses are invisible substances such as spirits and God. Along with substances, complex ideas also take the form of "mixed modes," which are abstract ideas and relations used to judge in moral, legal, and political matters. Mixed modes are human contrivances: "how remote soever they may seem from Sense, or from any operation of our own Minds, are yet only such, as the Understanding frame to it self, by repeating and joining together *Ideas*, that it had either from Objects of Sense, or from its own operations about them" (2.12.8). Together, substances and mixed modes encompass the categories for judging in natural, moral, and political philosophy. In making such judgments, however, humans have only fragmented and partial materials to work with, drawn from the evidence of nature and the testimony of others as well as Revelation. Whether seeking to understand the natural world for scientific pursuits or the law of nature for moral and political matters, we must interpret fragmentary evidence and make judgments amid uncertainty generated by plural viewpoints, partial observations, and inconstant communication, as well as the ability to think on possibilities that may or may not come before one's senses.[19]

Locke's claim to experience should not be understood as a denial of a vast terrain beyond the senses of the human understanding, whether that be spirits or microscopic particles.[20] Rather, it is precisely such broader views that one must cultivate to enable judgment, but that requires moving beyond sensory experience. For Locke, "Analogy in these matters is the only help we have, and 'tis from that alone we draw all our grounds of Probability." "[A] wary Reasoning from Analogy" is essential for judgment that is grounded in experience, but not limited to the sensible world. Analogy is important for Locke's account of how there must be beings leading from humans to God, just as experiments with the microscope revealed a world descending from humans, animals, and plants down to otherwise invisible particles: "Observing, I say, such gradual and gentle descents downwards in those parts of the Creation, that are beneath Man, the rule of analogy may make it probable, that it is so also in Things above us, and our Observation" (4.16.12). This structuring metaphor in Locke's thought is what McClure refers to as "God's Architecture," and it conforms to Brian Vicker's account of early modern rhetoric, in which the New Science is the occasion for enriching, rather than abandoning, analogies drawn from nature. In the same move, Locke affirms the value of analogy for scientific understanding as well as for religious thought.[21] Analogies not only sustain natural philosophy; they make for an enabling relationship of borrowing and lending between science and religion.

Analogy is essential to the ideas that humans can hold of divinity. The capacity of the understanding to meaningfully reflect on ideas of God and spirits depends not only on analogy from the scale descending down from humans, but also by analogy to their own internal perception: "[the mind] can have no other Notion of Spirit, but by attributing all those Operations, it finds in itself" (3.6.11). Humans are able to think on higher, spiritual beings by analogy with the last, highest observable creature, namely, themselves. In other words, humans can reflect on the idea of God, thanks to the trope of personification. As Philip Vogt writes, "Self-knowledge functions as the sole point of reference for the ascending intellect. . . . Through personification, theology as Locke understands it casts God in the image of man."[22] Such analogical thinking is not premised on a metaphysical claim about the essential similarity of the human understanding to spirits. On the contrary, it is the only means by which embodied creatures can reflect on what is beyond their senses. This important activity of the understanding relies on "borrowing from that which is familiar in order to name that which is elusive."[23] The plurality of ways that Locke figures God across his texts, for example, as father and maker, further attest to the rhetorical rather than essential nature of ideas of God.[24] Analogy is a mode of using experience to expand into the unfamiliar and the insensible.

Considering the distant and ineffable such as God, spirits, and the afterlife by virtue of analogy with sensory perceptions generates the force needed to inculcate new forms of mental relish. By borrowing images—for example, a human face for God or bodily pleasure and pain for the promises and threats of the afterlife—uneasiness and desire arise in relation to the ineffable such that they can rival everyday concerns. Analogy and personification offer the sense of grandeur and proximity needed to reorient human desires and actions toward the long view of the greater good. Through sensation, imagination, and memory, humans can give material force to formless ideas, rendering distant and abstract consequences vivid. Where a long tradition of sacred rhetoric practiced by the clergy achieved such effects of bringing closer and making vivid, here we see rhetorical figures associated with the individual's cultivation of mental relish or fashioning of the understanding in everyday practice.[25] For Locke, this is a matter of the conduct of the understanding for every person, no longer solely a special duty of a secular or religious authority. The reasonable conduct of the understanding depends on an orientation of one's desires toward long-term judgments concerning pain and pleasure. That reorientation is made possible by both the suspension of immediate judgment and the cultivation of new or alternative desires, made possible by rhetoric redeployed. In this way, the effective and inventive capacities of rhetoric are essential conditions for reasonable judgment in moral matters.

The Material Force of Language

Rhetorical figures structure other essential ways that humans draw from sensible and familiar experience to move beyond it. They include the range of categories and terms needed for organizing experience and judging, in natural and moral philosophy, law, and politics. Both substances and mixed modes such as general ideas and abstractions are, in turn, intimately bound up with Locke's account of language. Unlike his discussion of analogy, Locke does not name the rhetorical figure on which these ideas depend. Yet his account of the experiential origins of ideas that go beyond the senses are recognizable as metaphor and metonymy. This is perhaps Locke's most conflicted point of contact with the rhetorical tradition. He decries metaphor, even as he seems to depend on it. It is important to recognize the ways that this opposition to metaphor, combined with a praise for analogy, was common among Locke's fellow New Scientists. Analogy and metaphor are not so easily distinguished as these common claims suggest, however. As Vogt shows, the difference in Locke's writing is ultimately polemical rather than substantive.[26] With metaphor and analogy, we witness Locke's relationship of debt and denial to rhetoric. Just as Locke acknowledges the indispensable work of analogy for drawing from experience in the wake of skepticism, so too do metaphor and metonymy broadly serve his account of ideas and language in indispensable ways.

Taking up ideas of substances—whether a watch, a horse, or a human—Locke argues that humans may have a collection of sense perceptions of such entities, but there is no certainty to be had about their true essence. Rather, how to identify a substance depends upon its name and definition, that is, its nominal essence. God may create such entities, but humans author the words used to organize them. Our knowledge of what such substances are goes no deeper than this. The inessential nature of this practice is evidenced in the variety of ways that similar things can be defined, as well as the way that a word in one language may have no counterpart in another. Locke goes so far as to insist that where there are two different names there are two different essences, even if in another language they might be understood as the same (3.3.14). Even the category "human" is inessential as far as the understanding can perceive, as evidenced by the variety of definitions noted by Locke (3.10.17).[27] This human authorship involves selecting simple ideas, grouping them into a definition, and then tying the bundle together with a name (3.3.20, 3.6.29–30). This process of selecting out one or several particulars to stand in for the whole is metonymy, and it is inextricably bound up with language (or "names," in Locke's parlance).

With human knowledge limited to their nominal essences, substances always already involve thought in language. It is tempting to assume that such nominal essences are based on a pattern in nature because Locke says that nature provides a kind of archetype for them.[28] Rather than providing a stable foundation for language and natural philosophical concepts, however, this sense of an archetype is likely to mislead. Substances are *more* likely to draw humans into error than wholly invented complex ideas (3.6.40). Their dual qualities of nominal and inaccessible real essences make it easy to believe that our words for categories of things speak of the world as it is across time and place, when Locke argues that is not the case. The particulars associated with any given substance may originate in sensory perception, but they are transformed into general ideas and names of species or types of complex creatures and objects only through an underdetermined selecting of particulars and elevation of these particulars as paradigmatic. In other words, they are created as metonymy.

Even more than substances, the ideas under the heading of "mixed modes" are a matter of human invention. They are put together by the understanding and they acquire significance and duration once they are given a name. Included in these are general and universal ideas, which Locke calls the *"Inventions and Creatures of the Understanding,* made by it for its own use" (3.3.11). They depend on the combining and separating capacities of the understanding. More specifically, it is the repetition of a particular idea, stored in memory and recalled by imagination, that is then made to stand in for future cases. Locke gives an example of a general idea of white. While white is a simple sense perception, it becomes complex when we think of the color in general terms: "Thus the same Colour being observed to day in Chalk or Snow, which the Mind yesterday received from Milk, it considers that Appearance alone, makes it a representative of all of that kind; and having given it the name *Whiteness,* it by that sound signifies the same quality whereso-ever to be imagin'd or met with; and thus Universals, whether *Ideas* or Terms, are made" (2.11.9). General ideas, in other words, are no more than contingent particulars elevated to exemplary status, bound by the practice of naming. As Ernest Tuveson explains: "There is no need to use metaphor as a means of giving imagistic form to pure idea. The art of presenting the universal consists in the skill with which the writer or speaker selects the precise images which the mind will multiply, so to speak, into the general."[29] The relation between particular and universal in which the particular is selected to be used as a universal and applied to future cases is structured as metaphor and metonymy. While we have seen Locke attack metaphor as an abuse of language, here metaphor is incorporated into the very structure of ideas. As the example of whiteness suggests, this human work of elevating particulars is necessary in the creation of general ideas of all kinds, including in the study of the natural world as well as for use in the moral, legal and political realms.

In a similar manner, Locke suggests that abstractions emerge from a process of separating ideas from "all other Existences, and the circumstances of real Existence, as Time, Place, or any other concomitant *Ideas*" (2.11.9). To separate out a single idea in this way is to use a particular in a new way, in new relations. Abstraction for Locke too is generated through metonymy and metaphor. Its generality emerges when a particular comes to be used as a representative for other ideas, that is, in asserting its relation of analogy or similitude to other particulars. In this way, Lockean abstractions are not formless or ineffable. Rather, in Hannah Dawson's words, "Our embodied minds yearn for sensible marks with which to think. They do it neither easily nor well with insensible ideas."[30] Locke's account of abstract, general, and universal ideas depends on figural uses of particular, sensory ideas because humans are embodied, thinking creatures.

Like substances, mixed modes depend on language for their continued use and meaning. In turn, however, general ideas form the basis for Locke's theory of language. Locke's account of how the categories we use to order and judge across realms of human life (science, law, etc.) are based in experience that is inextricably bound up with language. Words, or "names," refer almost always to general ideas in the mind of the speaker, with the exception of proper names (3.3.4–5). If we are to speak intelligibly, we must invoke ideas formed by metonymy, metaphor, and analogy, in ways that can be shared with others. There is no experience so simple or sensory that it can be expressed without such general ideas and recourse to metaphor and metonymy. In this way, Locke prefigures Nietzsche's account of language in "On Truth and Lies in a Nonmoral Sense," as suggested by de Man.[31] Where de Man emphasizes that Locke enacts a theory of language as trope while disavowing rhetoric, here we find that Locke's dependence on rhetoric is compatible with, even necessary to, his claiming of experience. Locke's debt to rhetoric, in other words, is not an accidental failure but, rather, an essential component of his account of human judgment based in experience.

The tie between language and experience in Locke's thought runs even deeper than we have so far seen, and the importance of rhetoric extends along with it. Language itself has a material character that proves indispensable to human thought in a variety of arenas. Material words, Locke recognizes, make their way into our thoughts and even into the very fabric of the human understanding.[32] Words are "sensible Marks of *Ideas*" (3.2.1) and they serve two essential functions. The aurality of speech and the visibility of imprinted characters, that is, of writing, are mechanisms that help to fix ideas in one's own understanding and share them with others (2.18.3, 4.11.7). First, as aids to memory, they help us to record our thoughts, helping to build and preserve one's storehouse of ideas: "[t]he use Men have of these Marks, being either to record their own Thoughts for the Assistance of their own Memory" (3.2.2). By enabling retention of ideas, language is also essential to the continuity of the self over time, that is, to consciousness. For this reason, as Dawson explains, words, for Locke, are "fundamental to, rather than a mere copy of human understanding" (4.5.3).[33] Locke registers ambivalence on this point as he insists that words reflect ideas, yet he grants that humans generally think in language.[34] We will return to this tension below, but for now it is important to note that Locke acknowledges the role that language plays deeply within his account of ideas and consciousness.

Second, words enable us to lay out our ideas for others (3.2.2). They are the condition of making ideas, otherwise hidden, sensible to the world. By *sensible*, we should understand Locke to be indicating the sensory nature of language as visible or audible, but that sensory quality is also the necessary, but insufficient, condition of one's ideas making sense, that is, having meaning, for others. In other words, it is the force of language to render sensible that enables us to expand and alter ideas and words by claiming experience. The advancement of philosophy, science, and so forth depends on the use of sensible markers of ideas. Language is "the great Conduit, whereby Men convey their Discoveries, Reasonings, and Knowledge, from one to another" (3.11.5). Words are essential to the shared pursuit of philosophy, both established practices of disputation and the emerging experimental science. Just as the new experimental science required the vivid rendering of observations, aimed at producing "virtual witnesses," Locke recognizes that, practically speaking, ideas depend on material words as well.[35]

It is not only the materiality of words themselves but also, and especially, those "sensible words" used as figures that lend meaning to ineffable ideas. Metaphor is essential for generating new meaning within language. Words tied to sensory ideas can be transferred to ineffable ideas, mirroring the use of analogy and personification in ideas of God. Locke remarks:

> [H]ow great a dependence our *Words* have on common sensible *Ideas*; and how those, which are made use of to stand for Actions and Notions quite removed from sense, *have their rise from thence, and from obvious sensible* Ideas *are transferred to more abstruse significations*, and made to stand for Ideas that come not under the cognizance of our senses; *v.g.* to *Imagine, Apprehend, Comprehend, Adhere, Conceive, Instill, Disgust, Disturbance, Tranquility*, etc. are all Words taken from the Operations of sensible Things, and applied to certain Modes of Thinking. *Spirit*, in its primary signification, is Breath; *Angel*, a Messenger: And I doubt not, but if we could trace them to their sources, we should find, in all Languages, the names, which stand for Things that fall not under our Senses, to have had their first rise from sensible *Ideas*. (3.1.5)

Words bear the memory traces of the figural thinking from which they derive meaning, as captured by the rule of analogy.

As Locke continues in this passage, we also see the importance of metaphor in conveying the experience of one human understanding to others: "[T]hey were fain to borrow Words from ordinary known *Ideas* of Sensation, by that means to make others the more easily to conceive those Operations they experimented in themselves, which made no outward sensible appearances; and then when they had got known and agreed Names, to signify those internal Operations of their own Minds, they were sufficiently furnished to make known by Words, all their other *Ideas*" (3.1.5).[36] To speak of thinking, imagining, disturbing, and so forth— to speak, in other words, as Locke does in the *Essay*—requires the resources of borrowed words, or metaphor, no less than sensory perception. Locke reveals here the figural conditions of his own writing, as well as of the practice of examining the human understanding with others more generally.

Because one gives an account only of one's experience of one's *own* understanding, we need to borrow sensible words to communicate the results of this experiment to others (Locke's language recalls us to the common origin of experience and experiment). As William Walker argues, "Locke is here granting a positive epistemological function, a pedagogical function, to at least some of those borrowings which, even though *he* does not, the rhetoricians and Leibniz name as tropes. In short, he is claiming, as both Aristotle and Cicero do, that some tropes *instruct*." In the passage in the *Conduct* where Locke expressed most concern about the tendency of metaphor and simile to generate false understanding, he nonetheless gives approval to similes and allegories as well as "figured and metaphorical expressions" as useful for communicating "abstruse and unfamiliar ideas" to others.[37] Locke appropriates the materializing force of language and the inventive power of metaphor from the rhetorical tradition not in spite of his claim to experience but precisely because of it. Where sensory experience is impossible— in matters of abstract thought or in understanding the minds of others—we must use rhetorical figures because vivid images have force for sensory creatures. Therein lies their danger and their indispensable power for cultivating judgment. Although the advent of modern science and Locke's thought in particular are often associated with a break with the rhetorical tradition, we see here how rhetoric makes possible, if uneasily, Locke's authorization of experience as grounds for human judgment.

Entangling Language and Experience

Rhetorical figure is essential for Locke in overcoming the challenges raised by his theory of language more generally, a view that posits a deep skepticism about shared understanding between conversants. Just as Locke argues that complex ideas are not given directly to the understanding by God or nature, he also argues that it is mistaken to assume one's words correspond to things in the world or ideas in others' minds (3.2.4–5). Locke's claim that "[w]ords, as they are used by Men, can properly and immediately signify nothing but the *Ideas*, that are in the Mind of the Speaker" resembles a common and unremarkable claim that words reflect ideas (3.2.4). As Dawson shows, however, this claim is much more controversial than it may seem as it marks "a bold departure in early modern philosophy of language by driving a particularly deep wedge between language and the world and highlighting the meaning of the speaker rather than the word." The emphasis is on how the signification of words is limited to the speakers' ideas "and they can be Signs of nothing else" (3.2.8). Nonetheless, Locke does not abandon the prospect of accounting for how our words become meaningful (or significant, in Locke's terms) to us as sensible creatures.[38]

To speak intelligibly, words must "excite the same *Ideas* in the Hearer" (3.2.8). On the one hand, Locke's point is that such excitation cannot be taken for granted, as unintelligible speech or insignificant noise is a common, if often unrecognized, occurrence. On the other hand, "*there comes by constant use*, to be such *a Connexion between certain Sounds, and the* Ideas *they stand for*, that the Names heard, almost as readily excite certain *Ideas*, as if the Objects themselves, which are apt to produce them, did actually affect the Senses" (3.2.6). With repetition, the tie between word and idea becomes so strong as to cause ideas to flood into the understanding, not unlike sensory perception. As we have seen, material words and sensible metaphors are indispensable for the human understanding to *make sense* of otherwise insensible ideas. Now we see, however, that language as a social practice generates a force sufficient to rival that of the material world. Interestingly, this does not lead Locke to retreat from his claim to experience as Rorty's "veil of ideas" would suggest. Instead, it presses toward an alternative account of rhetoric and materiality.

Locke's understanding of the material force of language adopts and redeploys another notion central to the rhetorical tradition. For classical and Renaissance rhetorical writers, including Aristotle, Cicero, and Quintilian, "the capacity of language to excite ideas in us as our sensation of the world itself does is central to discussions in rhetorical tradition of *energeia, enargeia*, ocular demonstration, vivid illustration, figures of speech, imagery, and figures of thought." In this tradition, however, this property was specific to oratorical and literary usage. Locke's adoption of this capacity is remarkable for the way that he attributes the power "to excite ideas which have the vividness, intensity, actuality, or force of ideas excited by the world itself" to common usage. A special skill involving persuasive and tropological power, once reserve for the orator, here becomes a matter of common use.[39] In a sense, Locke democratizes the capacity to generate rhetorical force by embedding it in the everyday practices of ordinary speakers.

We can now see how Locke ties language to experience in more than one way. He posits sensory and reflective experience and ideas as prior to language, but he goes on to describe a much more complex, bidirectional relationship. Insofar as language depends on experience, it does so by virtue of an underlying rhetorical capacity for choosing exemplary particulars and forming complex ideas through metaphor and analogy. As a social practice, repeated over time, language takes on a force that cannot be easily distinguished from other sources of perceptual experience. As a result, Locke's account of language reveals enormous creative power, working from and with experience understood as sensory, reflective, passionate, and intersubjective. Such linguistic creativity and force reiterates familiar seventeenth-century concerns about language and sharply intensifies them. Specifically, these concerns center on the plurality of meanings that words can take on for different speakers as well as the power of words to shape our perception of the world. Locke is well attuned to the ways that speakers and listeners proliferate meanings and to the way that language comes to seem natural, even when it is conventional. Such naturalized ways of speaking and thinking are for Locke the source of great authority over the human understanding and therefore a source of one power (or many) over the desires, knowledge, and wills of others. In other words, language has the power to undermine independent judgment.[40]

Locke worries about the creative and pluralizing capacities of language, to be sure, but he also sees them as endemic to language. For Locke, unlike his predecessors, pluralizing and naturalizing forces of language can affect even well-intentioned speakers.[41] As with the passions and imagination, the materiality of language is both a resource and a source of unruliness. While words can and should aid both human understanding and society, they can also be the source of "Noise and Wrangling, without Improvement or Information; whilst Men take Words to be the constant regular marks of agreed Notions, which in truth are no more but the voluntary and unsteady signs of their own *Ideas*" (3.10.22). As aural and visual markers, language poses difficulties not altogether different from the materiality of objects. Locke's worry, as Dawson explains, is that "words, leading examples of sensible objects, shove 'moral and more abstract ideas' out of the mind."[42] That is to say, words, like sensations, are necessary but may also disrupt and distract the cultivation and practice of good judgment. They do so by drawing ideas into the understanding, overrunning the power to suspend desires and make considered judgments about the greater good. Moreover, this automated response to words calls bundles of ideas, tightly connected, into the understanding as if they were naturally connected, rather like association. The naturalizing effects of material words undermines the capacity to consider critically the human work of creating complex ideas and words, lending authority to such bundles of ideas and passions where perhaps none is due. To treat language as natural, or given, is to allow ourselves to be spoken for, to give up the critical capacity to consider the relation between the words we use and the sensory and reflective experience they are supposed to communicate. Such insignificant speech renders humans as mere parrots, for Locke (3.1.1).

Despite Locke's concerns that we are merely parroting common speech patterns, he does not aspire to reject or even tightly circumscribe common usage.[43] While Locke is concerned to improve specialized forms of language for philosophy, he is far more critical of technical uses than of everyday meaning. In fact, he insists that speakers generally adhere to conventional use: "[C]ommon use, by a tacit Consent, appropriates certain Sounds to certain *Ideas* in all Languages, which so far limits the signification of that Sound, that unless a Man applies it to the same *Idea*, he does not speak properly" (3.2.8). On the one hand, language is the product of human invention and agreement. We are each like Adam, in the sense that we retain the power of naming and ordering the world around us. On the other hand, we are more like Adam's children, who must consider the practices that have already been established and make good-faith efforts to avoid confusion (3.6.51). Situated as both founders of language and their heirs, humans retain the capacity to reinvent words based on experience, yet they do so under constrained conditions. Locke's theory of language shows how language is conventional and how it may be necessary to interrogate the meanings and definitions associated with familiar words. Locke writes these sections with the air of a reformer, hoping to improve the clarity of speech. If our language is a human contrivance, then it remains open to revision. Locke insists on this, but only in the rare and necessary case. Our use of language must always involve a care for social relations, that is, for language as "the great Instrument and common Tye of Society" (3.1.1). Such care requires attention to common use and to fair notice of when we seek to change conventional definitions. Moreover, we must keep in mind that to advocate a large-scale break with common usage, as his contemporary universal-language philosophers did, would mean a loss of the material force of language that enables words to excite ideas in others' minds. The material force of language proceeds from inventive activity, but it cannot proceed from constant, radical recreation of language because that would neglect the social and habitual dimensions of language.

It is the power of words to excite ideas and move passions—to move body and mind—that inspires the impassioned attack on rhetoric at the close of book 3. Not surprisingly, Locke's concerns about passions and eloquence are closely linked. Both the passions and figural language are indispensable to expanding the compass of the human understanding, that is, to generating the frameworks of judgment that encompass the long as well as the immediate view. The difference is not between reasonable judgment freed of passions, imagination, and language and that dictated by them. Rather, Locke emphasizes the difference between judgment based solely on the immediacy of experience (which may include associations and enthusiasms, materials words as well sensations and passions) and judgment in light of a plurality of possibilities, some more distant, some more vivid than others. Immediate desires and impressions may still direct the will, but not necessarily. Temporarily suspending immediate actions creates the space for considering plausible alternatives, alternatives that may prove to generate the greater uneasiness. As individual moral subjects, we bear responsibility for expanding our understanding to encompass a wider range of possible goods as well as for cultivating the relish for the distant, but lasting, notions of the greater good. None of this is possible without the inventive and materializing force of rhetoric that Locke borrows for his account of the understanding and language. In other words, the pluralizing and imaginative capacities of rhetoric are indispensable to the critical negotiation of the experiential grounds and conceptual frameworks of judgment.

Anxiety and the Possibility of Critique

Locke's debt to rhetoric for his theory of judgment grounded in a world that is both material and social generates anxieties that are not easily allayed, if they can be at all. We might then ask, How does Locke preserve a practice of judgment fixed on the greater good, that is, resistant to the closest uneasiness of either a physical or social nature? For Tully, Locke's practice of judgment is grounded in Revelation, a source of natural law that gives shapes to a series of otherworldly and earthly rewards and punishments to guide judgment. Lockean judgment on this account produces a subject subjugated to overlapping layers of law (divine, civil, and humanist), yielding a juridical subject.[44] For Douglas Casson, Locke's practice of judgment is grounded in a more experiential form of probable knowledge, such as the natural desires implanted in humans by God. By tending to the observable signs of nature (in both the worldly and the divine sense of nature), Lockean subjects develop reasonable conduct of the understanding through a project of self-mastery of desires (or will) and actions.[45] On both accounts, Locke's judgment is grounded by a moral and natural order in which the subject must cultivate practices of subjugation; in the first case it is by recourse to text and in the second it is to observable natural signs.

Locke's faith in a larger natural and divine order is not in question here. Yet the access that humans have to such order is put significantly in question by Locke himself. Revelation is subject to interpretation, where plurality of meanings are produced in everyday religious and political life in the seventeenth century (a fact amply demonstrated in the following chapter, on Locke's scriptural engagement with Robert Filmer). Moreover, the notion of an infinite being is not immediately accessible to embodied creatures, thus necessitating contingent modes of invention to give distant and ineffable ideas materializing force. Such images for the divine, if they are to have any force, must come not from any higher source but from experience of the human understanding itself that must then be developed into religious analogy. This is not to say that natural signs or holy texts are irrelevant but that they do not reside beyond, or outside, the practices of human invention working contingently from experience or from the requirements of interpretation and the plurality afforded by language on an ordinary basis.

To seek such a secure foundation in Revelation or nature in aspiring to a self-mastered subject is to set aside the inventive practices that Locke makes visible for the readers of the *Essay*. As Kroll reminds us, for Epicurean materialist writers, such performance of the conditions of the text—in the *Essay*, the conditions of human understanding itself—is no accident. It is central to the pedagogical project of the text. In light of this, we cannot simply set aside the many sources of disruption and unruliness that Locke puts before his readers. These are not solely problems for cultivating a reasonable understanding; they are also resources. The project of the *Essay* begins as a challenge to philosophical authority—a way of speaking of timeless, universal truths that commands the ideas in men's minds. Locke poses that challenge by recourse to disruptive examples of contingent difference, drawing on experience that is both sensory and social. The sensory, reflective, and passionate nature of the human understanding itself offers a source of disruption based on experience to the universalism of innate ideas. In its place,

Locke turns to perceptual experience and inventive activity to generate the frameworks needed to judge our actions and the world in which we live. Such frameworks are not immediately given to the understanding by nature or God. That does not undercut Locke's faith in this order or in his belief that humans live under obligations to judge well in terms of an ordered universe. It means that such judgment—whether scientific endeavor or moral duty—is never freed of its origins in the inventive and figural work of rhetoric. Moreover, it is rhetorical invention that enables us to make claims based on our experience in terms sufficiently sensible to persuade others to make changes in their use of words and ideas. As such, it involves an ineliminable element of contingency, plurality (that is not necessarily error), and an openness to revision. We know this because Locke has made visible the inventive activity, that is, the work of analogies, metaphors, and metonymies needed to make judgment from experience possible. In this way, Locke gives material form through writing to the inventive, figural activity that is constitutive of the reasonable conduct of the human understanding.

To see Locke's *Essay* as giving material form to the otherwise hidden activities of the understanding is to recognize the way that he inaugurates an ongoing mode of critical judgment. The images he provides of the understanding—whether the well-known metaphors of white paper and a camera obscura or less familiar images of a ship and a presence-room—constitute his own rhetorical activity in theorizing reasonable conduct within a social and political context that does not always recognize experience as a basis for claims to knowledge.* Moreover, his explanation of the origins of ideas and words in experience attune readers to the possibility that the ideas that we use to frame our judgments could be different, just as the words we use can be reformulated. Cases may arise, therefore, in which we bear the responsibility for staging a disruption in common practices of thinking and speaking, and ultimately of acting. It is from our own experience and our capacity to render it vividly to others that we are able to disrupt the rule of propriety in language when necessary.

To overemphasize the containment of the disruptive sources of sensation, passions, and other forms of experience in the self is to lose sight of this ongoing need to challenge philosophical and political authority. Locke's *Essay* does not simply show how human reason and action must conform to existing frameworks of judgment. He also shows how humans are called upon to generate those frameworks. This may not involve radical creativity. It may rather be invention as a mode of discovery, as with interpreting scripture. Even then, however, Locke

---

*On less well known metaphors of the Lockean understanding, see Vogt, *John Locke*, ch. 2

shows the indispensable work of generating meaningful and forceful frameworks of judgment that creatively borrow from sensible experience, potentially in a manner unguided by the past.

For those readers of Locke who rightly recognize the skeptical and creative forces at work in the *Essay*, it is common to assume that both the uncertainty and the creativity must be reined in, perhaps by self-mastery or by rational or religious foundations.[46] For Dawson, who carefully shows the creativity, plurality, and instability built into Locke's philosophy of language, such grounding or containment is never achieved. Rather, she suggests that the plurality and creativity of Locke's view of language threatens to undermine his political thought.[47] She turns to the *First Treatise* for evidence for her claim that Locke insists on the clarity of words against his opponent, Robert Filmer.[48] As we will see next, however, the *First Treatise* demonstrates precisely the capacity for plural and creative interpretation, namely, what Dawson calls Locke's "readerly" view of exegesis, as integral for Locke's critique of patriarchalism.[49] As the following two chapters will demonstrate, the capacity for invention that generates plurality and uncovers new possibilities may create anxieties for Locke in the *Essay*, but it is also indispensable for his practice of situated and inventive political critique. If anything, the creative power of Lockean critique comes more vividly into the foreground as Locke engages the images and idioms of his political rivals in the *Two Treatises of Government*.

4

FEMININE FIGURES AND THE RHETORIC OF CRITIQUE

The *First Treatise of Government* has traditionally resided in the shadows of Locke's classic the *Second Treatise*.[1] If not for the interest of feminist interpreters of the canon of political theory over the past three decades, the *First Treatise* might well have remained the much maligned sibling of Locke's classic political text. As a sustained and critical engagement with the question of patriarchal power in politics, Locke's text has taken on new significance for feminist political thought and contemporary political theory more generally. Yet feminist interpreters, critics and admirers alike, adhere to an account of Locke as champion of "the man of reason," a subject (seemingly) disembodied and untouched by the influence of passions, imagination, and rhetoric. These interpreters wrongly overlook Locke's extended engagement with the power of rhetoric in the *First Treatise*, an engagement that troubles the clear opposition of masculine reason and its feminine exclusions. Engaging figural language in the *First Treatise of Government* reveals how Locke's political critique proceeds by imaginatively showing the irrationality of Filmer's patriarchalism, not by stripping away rhetoric, but by undermining its universalist claims and reinventing those claims in new and terrifying guises. The Epicurean materialist dimensions of Lockean critique come to the fore in Locke's relentless assault on the language and imagery of Filmer's *Patriar-cha*. Locke's creative use of rhetorical figure and style emphasizes contingent and diverse experience to belie Filmer's claims and defamiliarize absolute paternal authority, such that it comes to seem foreign. In following the varied and novel effects of Locke's feminine and foreign figures, in particular, we find a practice of critique in which rhetoric, both its disruptive and creative capacities, is vital to the production of grounds for new political judgments.

Repetition and the Return of the First Treatise

Locke's *First Treatise* refutes Robert Filmer's defense of patriarchal authority, *Patriarcha*, so thoroughly that it seems nothing more could be said in defense of father-kings.[2] Locke's readers have often reported how boring and repetitive the project is, registering its "deep-seated and wearisome sameness."[3] Such dogged refutation may have been needed in the seventeenth century, but surely its relevance has waned with open defenses of patriarchal authority. The repetitive nature of the *First Treatise*, the complaint goes, makes it exhausting, exhaustive, and exhausted.[4] This tiresome quality seems to testify to Locke's dismissal of rhetoric as playing any part in his political critique.

Despite this reputation, there are those interpreters who have found the *First Treatise* to be significant for understanding Locke's political thought and especially its critical encounter with a justification for political order made, in Gordon Schochet's words, "in terms of familial symbols, which meant that political authority was identical with the rule of a father or patriarch over his family."[5] Given its attention to the symbolic interconnections of sexual difference, authority, and reason, the *First Treatise* becomes newly and especially significant for feminist political theory. For Melissa Butler, Locke's engagement with patriarchalism offers critical resources for feminism because his argument for the contractual basis of marriage and for maternal authority signals his "classic liberal faith in the ability of individual women to overcome" what he sees as their natural weaknesses.[6] What is valuable in Locke's thought, for Butler, is a logic of formal equality that can be extracted from the contingent inegalitarianism attributed to historical context. In a recent revival of Butler's argument, Jeremy Waldron urges Locke's readers today to extend the universal egalitarian aspects of the *First Treatise* where Locke, in Waldron's words, "flinched."[7]

Where Waldron sees a flinch, many critics see at best a shrug in Locke's abstract individualist account of reason and its seemingly genderless character. Carole Pateman, most notably, contends that Locke has more in common with his patriarchalist opponents because of the ways in which women are covertly excluded from the status of the rationally consenting citizen, a category actually limited to male heads of household.[8] While Locke's appeal to an abstract individual as the subject of politics seems to displace the foundations of patriarchal authority, his individualism turns out to be defined in "contrast with the womanly nature that has been excluded from civil society."[9] Adopting Genevieve Lloyd's use of "the man of reason" to describe Lockean individualism, Pateman places Locke within a long line of thinkers who cast masculine reason against a not fully rational female subject as well as social relationships and qualities cast as feminine.[10] Locke's engagement with Filmer, for Pateman, is important because it shows the logic of Lockean politics to depend on the exclusion of female subjects associated with embodied, passionate, and relational dimensions of human existence.

We gather from these interpretations two deeply opposed views of Lockean reason in relation to gender and authority. Locke's greatest value for feminist critique for Butler is precisely the source of his patriarchal tendencies for Pateman. Yet they have common ground in that their assessments of Locke's political thought turn on his "man of reason," an individual insulated from the influence of embodiment, passions, and social relations. This common ground returns us, as well, to those readers who too easily dismiss the *First Treatise* as tiresome repetition. Locke emerges repeatedly as a thinker who champions a notion of reason detached from and master over all other influences, whether that of the feminine powers of the passions and imagination or that of the persuasive powers of rhetoric. But this is not the only framework for interpreting the critical power of Locke's engagement with sexual difference, authority, and reason.

It is a testament to the power and limits of Pateman's argument, in particular, to take stock of the many interpreters that have sought to correct and expand her account of Locke's covertly gendered "man of reason."[11] For Barbara Arneil, Locke covertly excludes women not only as wives and mothers but as servants and slaves as well.[12] Nor are all of Locke's gendered exclusions covert, as Nancy Hirschmann shows through her intersectional analysis of the gender and class subordinations in his writings on education and the poor laws.[13] Yet as Terrell Carver demonstrates, none of these accounts fully engages the *multiple* overtly gendered depictions of authority and reason in the *Two Treatises*, including nursing fathers, warrior-like patriarchs, Queen Mary, and subordinate wives, to name a few.[14] What happens to the "man of reason" as masculinities and femininities proliferate, as they do so vividly in the *First Treatise?* Does the sexual binary that, for Pateman, structures Lockean reason still meaningfully organize the text or does the text come to organize gender, reason, and authority in unexpected ways?

I propose that we take the insight shared by Butler and Pateman that the *First Treatise* warrants deeper engagement and may still be alive to us as a political text. Yet I propose to do so by responding to the repetition of the *First Treatise* as a symptom of its debt to rhetoric. In doing so, I take up the plurality of gendered images in the text not only for what they say about actual men and women but also for *how* they function within Locke's political critique of Filmer.[15] Locke, as we will see, took very seriously the rhetoric of *Patriarcha*, and, in turn, we should take the rhetoric directed against *Patriarcha* to be no less important. This is to consider a new and more productive relation between Locke's reasoned refutation of Filmer and his critical refiguring of the images and idioms of patriarchal authority.

The transformative effects of rhetoric in Locke's *Essay* calls for a second look at the *First Treatise*, a text preoccupied with the power of rhetoric to persuade men into slavery. Tracing Locke's relation of debt and denial to rhetoric in the *First Treatise* will transform the way we understand his critique of patriarchal authority. While rhetoric certainly appears in Locke's text in the pejorative sense of "mere" persuasion, his use of tropes and figures evidences a more creative intervention into the politics buttressed by Filmer's *Patriarcha*. The figures and tropes appearing in Locke's political critique, as we will see, signal a broader project of re-presenting familiar images and idioms of patriarchal authority in newly unfamiliar and unsettling ways. Rhetoric, we will find, is no less essential to Locke's political critique than it is to his critique of philosophical authorities. As in the *Essay*, he draws upon figure and style to challenge overreaching universalism and reorient readers to the contingency and plurality of worldly experience. In examining his style and method of critique, we gain a new sense of the importance of the *First Treatise* as well as a new way of understanding his feminine figures.

Readers of the *First Treatise* may complain of boredom, but Locke insists that they should be afraid. Those who register a wearying sameness in the *First Treatise* overlook its strikingly dramatic re-creation of the patriarchal theory of authority of Robert Filmer. Locke begins the *First Treaties* with the charge that Filmer offers up a "strange kind of domineering Phantom." It is called "the *Fatherhood*" and it is of great value, for "whoever could catch [it], presently got empire, and unlimited absolute Power." This phantom figure seems to walk and talk, carrying itself throughout history, keeping the world in order from the time of the *Patriarchs* until the Flood. We see the phantom get out of the Ark with Noah and his sons, but there are some rough patches as "then the poor *Fatherhood* was under hatches, till *God by giving the Israelites Kings, Re-established the ancient and prime Right of the Lineal Succession in Paternal Government*" (1.6). Granting the occasional detour, the Fatherhood marches on through history. The Fatherhood, on Locke's recounting, is personified and peripatetic, surfacing everywhere and always.

While the language of the Fatherhood is drawn from *Patriarcha*, it does not function for Filmer as it does for Locke. The character of the Fatherhood as an agent with the capacity for possession (of authority, of empire) as it appears in the *First Treatise* is at least as much Locke's as Filmer's, if not more so.[16] So what is the figure of the phantom Fatherhood meant to signify for Locke? To briefly situate it in context, the phantom presents *Patriarcha* as a text and a political argument that will not remain buried. Written at least fifty years earlier, *Patriarcha* was published for a later generation of royalist supporters in 1680 and soon attracted Locke's attention.[17] Locke's choice of the phantom fatherhood image suggests a resurrected political argument, a text that has come back to live beyond its time.[18] As Charles Tarlton argues, the *First Treatise* does not simply take on the long-dead Filmer as its opposition. The threat that Locke addresses is those who take Filmer's ideas and seek to insinuate themselves through flattery to the ear of the monarch: this last generation of men "who would flatter princes with an Opinion, that they have a Divine Right to absolute Power" (1.3). In other words, the *First Treatise* aims not only at a refutation of Filmer's arguments but also at an attempt to "penetrate and disarm" the persuasive flattery of those who would convince the monarch of his absolute and arbitrary power.[19] Locke repeatedly criticizes Filmer's rhetoric as a source of tiresome, but dangerous, confusion and deception: "I have unavoidably been engaged in it by our A's way of writing, who hudling several Suppositions together, and that in doubtful and general terms makes such a medly and confusion, that it is impossible to shew his Mistakes, without examining the several Senses, where in his Words may be taken" (1.20; also 1.6, 13, 21, 110–111). The words, no less than the ideas, of royal absolutism are the central concern of the political critique of the *First Treatise*.[20]

Tarlton is right to draw our attention to how much of Locke's text exceeds the narrow refutation of minutiae for which it is famous, but there is much more to be said about the rhetorical dimensions of this text. Locke seeks to undermine a dangerously persuasive politics, but it is his own rhetoric that refigures a familiar guise of political authority. The phantom Fatherhood appears in Locke's text as a trope. The wandering personification of patriarchalism is a prosopopoeia, "a rhetorical figure by which an imaginary or absent person is represented as speaking or acting."[21] As trope, the phantom exhibits the rhetorical sleights of hand of which Locke continually accuses Filmer: "I observe not that he states the Question, or rallies up any Arguments to make good his Opinion, but rather tells us the Story as he thinks fit, of this strange kind of domineering Phantom" (1.6). Nonetheless, it is Locke who authors this trope. In choosing prosopopoeia, a personification that covers over an absence, Locke conveys the transient quality of his target, both its mobile and its insubstantial character. Readers of *Patriarcha*, this trope suggests, are deceived but the deception will be difficult to detect.

Locke emphasizes the particular challenge of Filmer's ideas over other defenses of royal absolutism because he has carried this argument the furthest.[22] It is the extremity as well as the popularity of *Patriarcha* that draws Locke's undivided attention: "for from him every one, who would be as fashionable as *French* was at Court, has learned, and runs away with this short System of Politics" (1.5).[23] The rhetorical force of Filmer's text is Locke's greatest concern. Like the French language, Filmer's language threatens to smuggle in its absolutist principles and obscure clear understanding of an English way of political authority. Filmer's text has shown itself capable of moving people through rhetoric to political conclusions that Locke seeks to challenge. Thus, Locke's challenge requires more than logic. It calls for an engagement with the affective and imaginative forces of rhetoric to dispel the specter of royal absolutism.

Locke's rendering of the Fatherhood as prosopopoeia points to his relation of debt and denial to rhetoric. The phantom implicates Filmer in deceptive rhetoric, while highlighting Locke's dependence on figure and trope to challenge patriarchal authority. Among the Fatherhood's most notable features is his detachment from the material world, namely, its history and topography, as well as from culture and social context. It wanders without bounds, seemingly everywhere and without alteration. It is, in a word, universal, yet the personification is a work of imagination covering over an absence. Locke shows readers the inventive work of rhetoric needed to produce Filmer's claims such that they come to be available for judgment. The Fatherhood figures a universalist claim to authority that is premised on absence and imagination, achieved through rhetoric. Locke then establishes himself as a critic of that universalism. While feminist critics of Locke have sometimes found affinity with him as a critic of patriarchy, few readers have recognized the affinity between Locke as a critic of a timeless universal conception of political authority and feminist critiques of the "man of reason."[24] It is this affinity that I will explore next through Locke's critical engagement with the patriarch as prosopopoeia.

Dismembering Patriarchalism/Remembering Authority

Filmer's *Patriarcha* is dangerous to Locke because it "would perswade all Men, that they are Slaves" (1.1) and set "the Foundation on which his absolute Monarchy stands, and from which it erects it self to an height, that its Power is above every Power" (1.6). The imaginary and rhetorical force of the phantom Fatherhood allows Filmer's idea of authority to rise to great heights and achieve the appearance of sovereignty. Challenging this image of authority requires the repetition of the *First Treatise*. Locke seeks to refute the foundation of Filmer's thought: the denial of natural freedom. But if this were solely a matter of demonstrating Filmer's errors, the *First Treatise*, as many readers have concluded, should have been considerably shorter. Read rhetorically, the repetition of the *First Treatise* no longer functions as just "wearying sameness." There is, instead, productive difference in Locke's repetition.

Locke excuses his repetition by attributing it to Filmer's evasive style of huddling and scattering his concepts and arguments. Where Filmer should be giving definitions so that readers "might have had an entire Notion of this *Fatherhood*," Locke accuses Filmer of evading objection "and clearing a Difficulty or two with one half Reason." Where there should be a complete notion, only one half appears: "God says, *Honour thy Father and Mother*; but our Author contents himself with half, leaves out *thy Mother* quite, as little serviceable to his purpose" (1.6). Filmer's theory lacks half its reason and all its maternal origins, Locke argues. Remembering the missing mother in these introductory remarks and throughout the *First Treatise* plays a central role in Locke's efforts to counter the rhetorical force of the patriarchalism by dismembering the phantom Fatherhood.

Locke's critique begins with the claim that there is an absence at the heart of *Patriarcha* and that absence is associated with the maternal. He returns to this absence throughout the book, showing in various ways that crucial phrase "*and Mother*, as Apocriphal Words, are always left out" (1.60). Locke does more than point to Filmer's omission, however. Much of the argument of the *First Treatise* depends on Locke's particular recollections of the mother that has gone missing from patriarchalism to show how Filmer's theory cannot stand once she has been restored. What matters here is not simply that he does so but *how* Locke effects this restoration of the mother to her rightful place. Locke's re-presentation of the missing mother goes well beyond making present what is absence. Maternal absence creates a space where Locke signifies the feminine, multiple times in different ways so as to subvert the unified and universal claim to authority of the Fatherhood. Where the Fatherhood is purportedly unitary and timeless, Locke's critical attack is generated through a contingent and plural femininity.

The alleged omissions and obfuscations of *Patriarcha* set for Locke the task of reconstructing Filmer's argument, piecing together the fragmented text and parsing out ideas and definitions from ambiguous passages. Locke's is an Epicurean materialist approach to interpretation as he summons his reader into the shared labor of reconstructing meaning: "Let us then endeavour to find what account he gives us of this *Fatherly Authority*, as it lies scatter'd in the several Parts of his Writings" (1.8). It is Epicurean materialism mixed with irony, however, as he establishes himself as exegete of Filmer's text as if it were scripture, undertaking a mode of interpretation for which Locke and those of his generation were well trained and deeply familiar.[25] His exegesis begins by laying out three parts to the argument of *Patriarcha*, that is, to the construction of the Fatherhood, centered on the figure of Adam as father, husband, and king: God's grant of dominion to Adam over the earth and its creatures, the dominion that God gave over Eve, and Adam's dominion as father over his children (1.14). Locke then turns his exegetical skills from *Patriarcha* itself to Filmer's chief source, the Bible, in order to recall Eve as a challenge to Filmer's portrayal of Adam as first king, first father, and first husband. Eve, in other words, is the first figure that Locke invokes to signify the missing mother, making visible what is lacking in the Fatherhood.

Taking on the Filmerian position that "[a] *Natural Freedom of Mankind cannot be supposed without the denial of the Creation of* Adam," Locke sets out to show that natural slavery cannot be supposed without denying the creation of Eve.[26] Adam is no "*Monarch Proprietor of the World*," because express donation of authority by God is conferred in the presence of both Adam and Eve (1.16). If it is a matter of who came first, "the Lion have as good a Title" as Adam (1.15). If it is by God's appointment of Adam, then there is no Adam without Eve. Human authority is conferred on two rather than one.

Locke goes on to contest Filmer's case that Adam's authority comes by fatherhood based on God's order to be fruitful and multiply and have dominion over "*every thing that creepeth on the Earth*." Locke examines the "express words" of this verse, especially the "one General Name" used by God, "*Living Creatures*" (1.25). He finds reptile, fowl, and sometimes cattle, but no humans within the biblical category of living creatures. Where Locke does find another human is in "the Plural Number" of God's addressees: "God blessed *them*." God spoke to Eve as well as Adam and that plurality of speech means that Adam's dominion is "in common with the rest of Mankind" (1.29). The introduction of Eve to Adam's dominion over other creatures delineates a distinctively human authority that is held in common. The figure of Eve recalls not only an originary woman but a more general human plurality, both of which the Fatherhood obscures.

Taking up Adam's supposed authority as husband, Locke turns to the curse on Eve after the Fall. He urges his readers to "consider the Force of the Text in hand" without leaping to Filmer's predictable conclusion: "[L]et *Rule* in any Text, be but once named, and presently *Absolute Monarchy* is by Divine Right Establish'd." Eve again figures centrally in Locke's return to the text, but this time, it is Adam who is introduced (back) into the scene. Scrutinizing God's words to "our first Parents," Locke emphasizes Eve's curse as no occasion for granting authority to an also disobedient Adam: "[H]e too had his share in the fall . . . and 'twould be hard to imagine that God, in the Same Breath, should make him Universal *Monarch* over all Mankind, an a day labourer for his Life." For Locke, Adam has "accidentally a Superiority" over Eve based on her proportionately greater punishment (1.44). Interpreting the curse as a shared condition, albeit with different punishments, enables Locke to situate the moment as one of contingency rather than universality. In other words, Eve's curse alongside Adam's is relevant as a judgment handed down upon these two in particular rather than a timeless condition of one sex over the other. Adam's authority over Eve, like Eve's authority over her children, is rendered particular once more as Locke goes on to contrast both with *political* authority: "If therefore these words [the curse] give any Power to *Adam*, it can be only a Conjugal Power, . . . the Power that every Husband hath to order the things of private Concernment in his Family . . . and to have his Will take place before that of his wife in all things of their common Concernment; but not a Political Power of Life and Death over her, much less over any body else" (1.48; also 1.49, 64). Where Eve was first introduced as a marker of particularity, here it is Adam and Eve who together disrupt Filmer's patriarchal universalism.

The passages under consideration here in which Eve is used as a foil for patriarchalism serve as important evidence for Locke's views on the status of women, but they do not settle the question of how we tell Locke's flinch from a shrug.[27] Rather than settling the question of the intentions behind these claims, we should follow the rhetorical gestures within these passages. Eve certainly can be read as a sign for all womankind. Indeed, Locke plays on the audience's willingness to read her this way (1.47). Yet she sometimes stands for much more when Locke situates her as a representative of human plurality as such. Other times, she stands for considerably less than womankind, representing the individual as subject of punishment. Locke's ambivalence with regard to Eve testifies instead to the broad range of rhetorical work that this feminine figure accomplishes for his political critique by refiguring the relation between universals and particulars in claims of authority, that is, by substituting and pluralizing the particular images that lend meaning to Filmer's timeless universal claim of patriarchal authority.

Situating Adam and Eve as similar in their grant of authority and subjection to punishment, Locke renders Adam and thus the Fatherhood as particulars, like Eve. This pluralizing force of the figure of Eve is integral to Locke's critique of Filmer's unified and unlimited depiction of sovereignty. Yet it is, at the same time, the particularity of Eve's condition and curse that Locke uses to separate out the shared original authority from political authority. It is against a threat of *unfettered* pluralization of political authority that Locke makes this separation. Were Eve's subjection to be seen as the universal origin of government, "there will be as many Monarchs as there are Husbands" (1.48). To accept Filmer's single figure of authority yields the unlimited proliferation of authority everywhere, according to Locke. Pluralizing new images of authority, Locke effects a reversal in which Filmer's single figure of authority yields unlimited reproductivity. Unyielding repetition remains at issue in the *First Treatise*, but whose?

Locke's critique of *Patriarcha* does not simply reveal Filmer's inconsistencies. It transforms the image of the whole of authority into a larger and differentiated set of particular figures of authority (parental, conjugal, human, masculine, feminine). Paired with Eve in her various significations, the timeless, universal image of patriarchal authority comes to appear as metonymy, a trope in which a part comes to stand for the whole. By recalling the apocryphal mother, Locke refigures the image of the whole of authority here such that the father is merely one of several kinds of authority. Resituated alongside Eve, the Fatherhood now appears as lacking. Locke's use of Eve as the missing mother does not secure a place for women as figures of political authority (1.48), but it has the effect of locating absence at the heart of the Fatherhood. In this way, Locke comes to *refigure* the image of patriarchalism.

As we now see, Locke's reworking of patriarchal authority through various rhetorical tropes does more than poke holes in Filmer's logic. Pluralizing images of authority through the figure of Eve, Locke presents patriarchalism as prosopopoeia and then highlights the metonymies that compose it, revealing its shifting, partial character. Insofar as this depends on Eve as a supplement to patriarchal authority, at once necessary and displaced, an affinity emerges between Locke's challenge to Filmer's universalism and Pateman's challenge to Locke's.[28] Both seek to make visible the missing wives and mothers suppressed by their opponents' seemingly universal account of authority.[29] This is not to suggest that Locke offers a satisfactory account of political authority that could respond to feminist claims. Rather, his political critique in the *First Treatise* reveals a debt to rhetoric for enabling his challenge to a universalist claim to political authority by showing it anew in relation to the missing mother.

Parody and Paternity

The pluralizing effect of Eve as feminine figure is indispensable to Locke's critique of patriarchalism. Locke's work of refiguring patriarchalism is hardly finished, however. Feminine and masculine, especially paternal, figures continue to proliferate in the *First Treatise*, vividly revealing Locke's dependence on creative rhetoric to further his political critique.

The Fatherhood, Locke tells readers, wanders through time and across the globe. Indeed, the figure of patriarchalism travels within the pages of the *First Treatise* as well. Following the wanderings of the Fatherhood, the domineering figure emerges from Locke's pages as satire. By characterizing Locke's text as satire, I mean that it targets its "object of attack" with "wit or humor founded on fantasy or a sense of the grotesque and absurd."[30] Moreover, engaging this object of attack by imitation, Locke's satire also parodies.[31] Drawing on these styles for political critique, Locke inhabits and transforms the language and images of paternal authority out of which political claims to royal absolutism are constituted. Locke's use of satire and parody, I argue, are not simply literary flourish. They make up much of the critical thrust of Locke's argument against Filmer, further rendering the Fatherhood not only particular but also grotesque and absurd.

Judging from the political and rhetorical culture of the late seventeenth century, Locke was no stranger to satire and parody and the *First Treatise* bears this out.[32] We have already seen the first signs of parody in Locke's self-appointment as exegete of Filmer's fragmented and elusive text. This doubling continues and gets more serious when Locke's exegesis turns to Filmer's scriptural sources as well. This parodic strategy continues with the proliferation of images of both mothers and fathers to rival the unitary Fatherhood. As we know, the figure of Eve pluralizes images of authority, but Adam and Eve are not the only figures of parental authority on which Locke draws. The Fatherhood draws authority from his role as maker of children (1.52). Locke invokes a higher maker, God the father. *Making* children, on Locke's account, is "[t]o give Life to that which has yet no being, is to frame and make a living Creature, fashion the parts, and mould and suit them to their uses, and having proportion'd and fitted them together, to put into them a living Soul" (1.53). God, not human fathers, is the ultimate maker of human life, and therefore any such authority resides solely with the divine. Resituated in this way, Filmer presumes too much authority for human fathers, recasting the Fatherhood as a rival to divine authority.

Locke effects this transformation of patriarch into apostate by recourse to another maternal figure, this time the agent of reproduction favored by proponents of the New Science. The Fatherhood eclipses not only God's role as maker but the active role of mothers as well. It is she, Locke suggests, who nourishes "the child a long time in her own Body out of her own Substance" (1.55). While this argument seems obvious today, such assumptions were not so secure in the seventeenth century. Locke associates Filmer with an older Aristotelian tradition in which the father plays the active part in reproduction and the maternal role is either passive or aberrant.[33] By contrast, Locke forwards a newer view, in which the mother plays an active role in childbearing.[34] The missing mother here is replaced by another, especially materialist, feminine figure: the active maternal body of the New Science. Compounding the effect of the figure of Eve, the maternal body too recalls the double origins of parental authority.[35] Experimental science as well as scripture provide figures of the feminine that Locke invokes to displace patriarchal authority.

The Fatherhood comes to be positioned in contrast to the ultimate paternity of God the Father, on the one hand, and the shared parental agency of fathers and mothers, on the other. God figures as the original maker of human life, working through the bodies of mothers and fathers "to frame and make a living Creature . . . and having proportion'd and fitted them together" (1.53). Where God is the author of life, Filmer authors a figure of the undead, as Locke's pointed contrast between God's authorship and the Fatherhood's provenance shows: "But perhaps Sir *Robert* found, that this *Fatherly Authority*, this Power of Fathers, and of Kings, for he makes them both the same . . . would make a very odd and frightful Figure, and very disagreeing, with what either Children imagine of their Parents, or Subjects of their Kings, if he should have given us the whole Draught together in that Gigantic Form, he had painted it in his own Phancy" (1.7). Filmer's creation, an amalgamation of fathers and kings, makes not a living soul, but rather a monstrous production. The gigantic form, composed of improper parts and proportions, offends aesthetically as well as politically. The workmanship of God instills a living soul in its proper form, suited to its uses, while Filmer's workmanship yields a deceptive and monstrous figure of the walking dead. Locke here doubles the images of fatherhood, which newly casts Filmerian patriarchy as outsized and threatening.[36]

This oversized Fatherhood is a theme that repeats and builds over the course of the *First Treatise*. Having doubled the patriarchal Fatherhood with God the Father, Locke goes on to depict its overreaching and excessive nature in striking images of transgression. In addition to this fearsome and gigantic form, the Fatherhood comes to be associated with another kind of patriarch: cannibal fathers. Locke makes this argument initially as the logical consequence of Adam's private dominion over all other creatures, including humans (1.27). This deduction takes new and vivid form, however, when Locke challenges the patriarchalist assertion that absolute paternal authority over children is affirmed by known practices of selling or exposing one's children (1.56). Filmer is not the only one to offer a story, however. Locke recounts at length the story, taken from Garcilaso de la Vega, of a people in Peru who "begot Children on purpose to Fatten and Eat them." Locke tells readers, "The Story is so remarkable, that I cannot but set it down in the A——'s Words." He goes on to quote:

> "In some Provinces, *says he*, they were so liquorish after Mans Flesh, that they wou'd not have the patience to stay till the Breath was out of the Body, but would suck the Blood as it ran from the Wounds of the dying Man; they had publick Shambles of Man's Flesh, and their Madness herein was to that degree, that they spared not their own Children which they had Begot on Strangers taken in War: For they made their Captives their Mistresses and choisly nourished the Children they had by them, till about thirteen Years Old they Butcher'd and Eat them, and they served the Mothers after the same fashion, when they grew past Child bearing, and ceased to bring them any more Roasters, *Garcilasso de la vega hist. des yncas de Peru*, I.1.c.12." (1.57)[37]

Locke spares no gruesome detail of the blood sucked from still-breathing bodies, feeding children begotten by mistresses who were "Strangers" captured in war. Augmenting the horror, the passage concludes in the butchering of these mothers' own children once they come of age served up alongside their mothers, who have outlived their reproductive purposes. Unlimited patriarchal authority is depicted here in striking images of transgression of the boundaries of family, society, and humanity.

Locke draws on the literature of European travel and conquest to dramatically refigure the terrain on which his readers encounter the absolute authority of fathers. We can think intersectionally about these images. Patriarchal fathers are figured here as foreign and savage in far more extreme terms than the French aspersions cast at Filmer early in the *First Treatise*. Like Eve, these foreign figures serve to challenge Filmer's patriarchalism. There are, however, important differences in the way that Locke's gendered figures signify patriarchal authority and its absences and exclusions. Unlike Eve, the Peruvian cannibals challenge conjugal and parental relations. The men are described mixing with foreign captives who bear their children only to be sacrificed and eaten later. This practice also marks a failure to generate a legacy, as their progeny are eaten by the age of thirteen. These images contrast sharply with that of Locke's Eve, who marks a relatively unobtrusive component of parental authority while remaining an outsider to political authority.

There is a politics to Locke's refiguring of patriarchal authority through feminine and foreign figures as particulars. Locke signifies femininity and foreignness through intersecting images of women as mothers and wives and indigenous men and women as perpetrators and victims of barbaric cannibalism. Insofar as these figures remain relegated to a position excluded from civil society and political authority, we find further evidence affirming the findings of Pateman, Arneil, Hirschmann, and Carver that Locke harbors a residual, racialized patriarchalism.

Without discounting such residual patriarchalism, to stop at this conclusion misses what is most powerful in Locke's critique. In their respective ways, these figures of femininity and foreignness are essential to Locke's critical refiguring of the Fatherhood by revealing its excesses and absences. The figures of Eve, the Peruvian cannibals, and the maternal body of the New Science all function, in differing ways, to transform the way we perceive Filmer's universal. Specifically, their rhetorical effects refigure a timeless universal into politicized particulars. As we will continue to see, it is the particulars that come to transform the universal rather than the universal that determines the particular. We may not find Locke's figures positioned as universal, but these particular figures importantly carry the force to transform and dismember Filmer's universalism.

Locke's cannibal tale reveals important limits to Locke's political imagination concerning female and foreign subjects, but that is not all it does. The cannibal tale also reflects on the power of human imagination more generally and paves the way for even stranger depictions of patriarchal power. Locke associates absolute authority in the case of the Peruvian cannibals with the unbounded possibilities of human imagination and convention: "Thus far can the busie mind of Man carry him to a Brutality below the level of Beasts" (1.58). There is, Locke suggests, no limit to what precedent can support, as this tale from the Americas testifies. The world, as he shows, includes practices more barbaric than the Fatherhood's select roamings encompass.[38] Although Locke styles himself as the champion of reason here against unbounded imagination and custom, we should not be blinded by the remarkable reimagining of patriarchal fatherhood as foreign, lawless, and driven by unfettered and licentious appetites. While imagination may carry men to unknown depths, it is the power of Locke's imaginative rhetoric that pushes forward his critique of patriarchal authority. Indeed it is only his inventive rhetoric that could refigure patriarchal authority into the unfamiliar and counterintuitive depictions that come next.

A central conceit of the *First Treatise* is that the Fatherhood is Filmer's creation. Yet the Fatherhood advances to greater and greater heights of lawlessness and transgression, to the point of grotesque absurdity. We give Locke at once too much credit for textual fidelity and too little credit for rhetorical force if we overlook the way that he critically refigures the words and ideas of *Patriarcha* for effects that are absurd and revolting. But what political work does Locke's satiric rendering of the Fatherhood as grotesque and absurd accomplish? What are the stated or implicit norms that Locke's satire is meant to achieve?[39] To accept Filmer's historical evidence that "[a]nciently, it was *usual* for Men *to sell and Castrate their Children*," is, for Locke, to justify adultery, incest, and sodomy. Such practices "cross the main intention of Nature, which willeth the increase of Mankind, and the continuation of the Species in the highest perfection, and the distinction of Families, with the Security of the Marriage Bed, as necessary thereunto" (1.59). Cannibalism and castration, like adultery and sodomy, are cast as sins against the family and its capacity to reproduce within the security of the marriage bed. In other words, patriarchal authority, for Locke, is dangerous because it interferes with the capacity to produce legitimate heirs.[40] In a strange twist, Locke argues a politics of the family to which patriarchal fathers are rendered outlaws.

Where the traditional political concern over inheritance would center on the number of sons as claimants to the throne, Locke effects a reversal by which the Fatherhood produces too many fathers. For if paternal right "does give *Royal Authority* . . . there will be as many Kings as there are Fathers" (1.70) and as many monarchs as there are husbands. Locke's concerns about the security of the marriage bed reveal that this proliferation of monarchs is not contained by the household. Without express and legal ties between mothers and fathers, Locke suggests, fathers reproduce unnaturally and without limit (1.72). This strange and vivid rendering of patriarchal authority culminates in a list, counting no fewer than fourteen claimants, yet not one an heir. All patriarchal authority produces are bastards. Yet the Fatherhood issues not sons, but bastard-fathers. The Fatherhood is at once cast in terms of uncontrolled fecundity and as "this *New Nothing*" (1.72), incapable of yielding a true heir.[41] The Fatherhood is at once fertile and barren, totally dominating the family and thereby destroying it.

It is no surprise to find the question of inheritance—political and familial—at the heart of the *First Treatise*, a document undertaken amid the Exclusion Crisis, which can itself be seen as a crisis of inheritance.[42] For those who find only the "man of reason" in this text, however, it should come as a surprise to encounter the rhetorical work of inventive refiguring at the heart of Locke's critique of royal absolutism. To gain a better sense of how the *First Treatise* situates Locke within a rhetorical as well as political culture, consider a contemporaneous but politically oppositional text by John Dryden, a fellow member of the Royal Society. His satirical political poem "Absalom and Achitophel" was dubbed by Richard Ashcraft "one of the most powerful political poems ever written."[43] Dryden's forceful attack on the Whigs and Shaftesbury, in particular, also centers on questions of paternal authority, royal promiscuity, and inheritance, yet it offers a striking counterimage to the simultaneously fecund and barren Fatherhood. While Dryden's king, like the Fatherhood, is at the center of a crisis of succession, it is the failure of women's active role in reproduction and a "viper-like . . . mother plot" that threatens the monarchy.[44] Dryden's maternal monstrosities are deployed in a royalist defense where Locke's monstrous fathers serve the cause of Exclusion. In other words, Locke's monstrous Fatherhood draws from and participates in a rhetorical culture in which transforming familiar images of authority—conjugal, parental, and political—through satire and parody constitutes serious political critique.

We do not have to ascribe to Locke the poetic talents of a Dryden to recognize the indispensable work of rhetoric in the *First Treatise*. We simply need to recognize the ways in which particular rhetorical figures and styles are fundamental to producing the meaning of political theoretical arguments. As Ashcraft argues, political theory should be seen as a "social language" that flows through diverse modes of political and literary forms.[45] Not only is there political significance to be found in literary texts, but, as the *First Treatise* demonstrates, the meaning of a political text is constituted through its rhetoric. In precisely this way, Locke recasts the Fatherhood as the object of satire. Through satire, he effects a dramatic transformation of the Fatherhood by moving from familiar images of royal authority, familial order, and primogeniture to cast patriarchalism as a threat to familial and political order. Far from being merely incidental to the *First Treatise*, the simultaneously fecund and impotent Fatherhood is at the core of Locke's critique of royal absolutism. More specifically, Locke's critical intervention by parody and satire discloses a new and impossible image of the Fatherhood that renders claims to universal patriarchalism unreasonable and unpersuasive. In this way, Locke's critique proceeds as an inventive reimagining of Filmerian patriarchy, a case against absolutism that cannot be conceived without rhetoric.

Locke's Critical Inventions

We may well wonder, after all, how it is that the *First Treatise* garnered its reputation for wearying sameness after such tales of the wandering undead, cannibalistic rituals, and castrating fathers. What was taken as repetition now emerges as symptomatic of the essential work of rhetoric in Locke's critique. It may be tempting, however, to see Locke going to such absurd lengths to dissolve Filmer's argument into "mere" rhetoric only to contrast it with his own universal based in reason, bringing us back to the old opposition between (Locke's) reason and (Filmer's) rhetoric. But this would only capture half of what we have so far seen in the *First Treatise*. Locke reveals the rhetorical and imaginative conditions of Filmer's universal claims by using particulars drawn from stories of scripture and travel as well as materialist facts from experimental science. Even more, however, we find that Locke's stories and figures, especially those foreign and feminine, transform the idioms and images of patriarchal authority, such that Filmer's own text cannot be read the same way again. Locke does not merely deny Filmer's claims as much as refigure them, meaning that Locke's argument is not captured by a philosophical framework that emphasizes truth and falsehood, such as we would expect from the "man of reason." Instead, the novel and impossible images of the Fatherhood generated through Locke's feminine figures create new possibilities for political contestation because they reinvent the image of fathers as kings and kings as fathers that sustains patriarchal authority, in public and private life. Locke engages and challenges the symbolic order of political and familial authority on which patriarchalist claims to authority depend. Moreover, he appropriates and redeploys these images *from within* this cultural frame in order to inventively transform its meaning for a particular audience.

There is no doubt that Locke sees himself as having reason on his side, but, as I have shown, this need not entail a rejection of rhetoric. In fact, Locke could not generate such a forceful critique without inventive rhetoric because that is the capacity to take familiar images and idioms from common political experience and transform them into something wholly other. When Locke presents the Fatherhood as prosopopoeia, then as metonymy and finally as object of parody and satire, he makes vivid the contingency of this mode of political authority, situating the Fatherhood as just one particular among many possible images of parental, conjugal, and political authority. In this way, he also inventively reveals new relations of similitude between maternal and paternal authority. Locke opens up a new space in which the Fatherhood, no longer the singular image of the universal, can now be related and compared to these other images of authority. He thereby challenges the continuous reproduction of the singular image of fathers as kings throughout history and around the globe. Pluralizing and decentering the patriarch, in this way, Locke opens new space out of familiar images and idioms, one in which not only the validity but also the very meaning of patriarchalism is newly open to question.

Locke's foreign and feminine figures re-present the once familiar image of the father-king from a very different perspective, now unfamiliar and threatening. Although these figures testify to Locke's limited imagination of gendered and raced subjects, they wreak havoc with a powerful convention of associating fathers with an authority that is at once political and familial. What Locke achieves is much more powerful than a simple denial of the truth of patriarchal authority. Skillfully presenting the Fatherhood as indistinguishable from figures of femininity and foreignness, Locke sets the very language of *Patriarcha* against itself, inhabiting, doubling, and redeploying the language of fatherhood in ways that unravel patriarchal authority from within. Locke's richly rendered, plural images of the other side of paternal authority—its maternal and indigenous others—deploy the disruptive power of imaginative language to subvert the continuous and boundless claims of patriarchal authority. We find in the *First Treatise* that the unruly creativity of language that Dawson sees as threatening to undercut Locke's political thought is instead the very capacity that enables the force of his critique.

5

THE MATTER OF CONSENT

Both Locke's *Essay* and the *Second Treatise* are centrally concerned with the nature of reason in individual and collective life. Yet such concerns with reason have historically been seen as separating rather than drawing the texts together, casting the "tabula rasa" as, in Laslett's words, "perhaps, the most effective solvent of the natural-law attitude."[1] In this way, the *Second Treatise* can seem like a departure not only from the *Essay* but, as we now see, also from the critique of patriarchalist universalism of the *First Treatise*. The question before us, then, is whether rhetoric recedes from the more affirmative political vision that has made this text a classic of political theory. It is here in the *Second Treatise*, where neither experience nor rhetoric seems to have much presence, that it is most challenging to locate the Epicurean materialist practices and conventions that we have identified in the other texts. Rereading this political classic with Locke's claim to experience and his debt to rhetoric in mind, we will uncover distinctly materialist and rhetorical dimensions that transform our understanding of Locke's practice of political critique for political subjects as well as theorists.

To suggest that the "two Lockes" are bridged by an Epicurean materialism centered around probable judgment based in experience that relies on rhetoric raises important questions that are elided by an emphasis on religion or reason as stabilizing external grounds of judgment.[2] As we have seen, the limited compass of the understanding, with its need for, and vulnerability to, sensory input, spurs of the passions, and material words complicates appeals to these foundations for judgment. We must consider more seriously how experience, in its rich, unruly, and manifold forms as sensory, passionate, and rhetorical, generates the conditions for judgment, particularly in a political order that hinges on individual consent.

One of Locke's most important and protodemocratic contributions to political theory is his notion of consent as the condition of legitimate authority. With consent, he elevates a speech act as origin of political authority and its absence as a legitimating condition for resistance. There is an underappreciated significance of both language and silence in the *Second Treatise* that signals the important work of rhetoric in Lockean political critique. We can understand this, however, only by taking up the challenging question of how the creative and disruptive power of language that we saw theorized in the *Essay* and put into action for purposes of critique in the *First Treatise* has anything other than, in Hannah Dawson's words, "a potentially devastating effect" on the speech act that institutes political community and authority.[3]

Political Origins, Consensual and Anthropological

The central place of judgment that we observe in the *Essay* finds its political correlate in the notion of consent and the possibility of resistance in the *Second Treatise*. In chapters 2 through 4, Locke lays down what seems a fairly simple distinction between consensual and nonconsensual conditions. It is consent, not birth, that places individuals in political society: "But I moreover affirm, That all Men are naturally in that State [of Nature], and remain so, till by their own Consents they make themselves Members of some Politick Society" (2.15). Authority absent consent signals an absolute authority that exceeds its acceptable limits, delineated by the bounds of self-preservation: "For I have reason to conclude, that he who would get me into his Power without my consent, would use me as he pleased, when he had got me there, and destroy me too when he had a fancy to it: for no body can desire to *have me in his Absolute Power*, unless it be to compel me by force to that, which is against the Right of my Freedom, *i.e.* make me a Slave" (2.17). The natural law of self-preservation delimits acceptable conditions for humans to live under (2.6), but it is consent or its absence that signals whether that standard has been violated. Political liberty, or "The *Liberty of Man, in Society*" remains contingent on consent to, and trust thereby placed in, the legislative power of the commonwealth (2.22). The judgment of individuals and of the society they form holds together only insofar as this consent and trust remain in place. Herein lies the distinction between free subjects and slaves: "[f]or a Man, not having the Power of his own Life, *cannot*, by Compact, or his own Consent, *enslave himself* to any one, nor put himself under the Absolute, Arbitrary Power of another, to take away his Life, when he pleases" (2.23). Consent marks a division between societies as political or not, between authority figures as absolute or limited, and between subjects as free and the enslaved.

The clarity of these distinctions in the first few chapters seems to lay out a seamless path to chapter 19, where Locke defends the right of resistance only after "a long train of Abuses, Prevarications, and Artifices, all tending the same way," has revealed a lasting transgression of these boundaries (2.225). The path between founding consent and the revocation of consent before faithless authority turns out to be a long train indeed, one with far more winding turns and stops than we might expect. In fact, the discontinuous style of the *Essay* and the repetitions of the *First Treatise* can be found in the *Second Treatise* as well, precisely in the origins of political authority as recounted by Locke in the chapters that follow these seemingly simple outlines of freedom and slavery in terms of consent and its absence. As with the texts we have already examined, the repetitions and disruptions surrounding Locke's notion of consent will be the starting point for a more careful examination of the rough ground of experience and the importance of material words as the grounds of critique.

The critical significance of Locke's claim to experience in the *Second Treatise* requires a closer look at the chapters that follow those brief, early accounts where we find Locke's political anthropology. To use a term applied by modern readers of Locke, the *political anthropology* identifies the references he makes to political authority gradually emerging out of familial and customary relations. These references to political origins seem, at first glance, to confound rather than complement the better-known notions of consent, compact, and resistance for which the book is famous. In light of the significant place of rhetoric in Locke's claim to experience in the *Essay* and in his political critique of the *First Treatise*, we can understand his use of political experience in the *Second Treatise* in a new way. We are now poised to find Locke grappling with the power of customary and affective ties in politics, not simply in order to dismiss or control them. While potentially troubling, political passions and social practices are also essential to a proper understanding of human judgment and political action, in particular to the possibility of political resistance. Reading the *Second Treatise* attuned to the rhetorical power of the political anthropology as a critical claim to experience brings into focus Locke's sustained interest not only in the unfreeing dimensions of the past but also in *how* we experience our shared political practices and history. In confronting the challenge of relating differently to the past, Locke relies upon the pluralizing and inventive power of rhetoric for enacting political critique.

Locke's political anthropology includes both a number of examples and a longer narrative account of the beginnings of political societies. As we have seen in his other texts, he draws from travel literature, history, and scripture to provide these examples, which serve diverse aims of the text. Some of these examples provide evidence to refute objections that a state of nature never existed or that a consensual founding moment never occurred. Other examples work with the longer narrative to suggest, by contrast, that hereditary monarchies likely originated in paternal authority.[4] The longer narrative of political origins is not as clearly located geographically or textually as are the examples, instead situated vaguely in the past: in the first ages, in the beginning, in a golden age. Interpreters of the political anthropology vary in their treatment of the anthropology as primarily composed of the examples versus the narrative, some emphasizing a single story line, while others highlight the diversity of examples of historical and cultural practices.[5]

Scattered discontinuously over chapters 6 through 8 of the *Second Treatise*, the narrative of the political origins of early societies does not conform to the more familiar version of people living in a state of natural freedom and equality until they consent to join together in civil society and establish standing, known laws, and common, impartial judges (2.4, 22, 87). While Locke frequently asserts that political authority is different from parental authority, he seems to make an exception when he writes in chapter 8, "*Of the Beginning of Political Societies,*" "I will not deny, that if we look back as far as History will direct us, towards the *Original of Common-wealths*, we shall generally find them under the Government and Administration of one Man. And I am also apt to believe that where a Family was numerous enough to subsist by it self, and continued entire together, without mixing with others, as it often happens, where there is much Land and few People, the Government commonly began in the Father" (2.105). Here, Locke hearkens back to an origin in familial relations that became political with no clearly recognized break between a social but prepolitical natural state and the institution of political community. This passage is not an isolated case. Speaking of paternal power two chapters earlier, Locke describes these "first Ages of the World" when humans tended to congregate in small family groups and fathers took responsibility for judging and punishing on behalf of their families even after the children grew to adulthood (2.74). Locke explains, "[T]was easie, and almost natural for Children by a tacit, and scarce avoidable consent to make way for the *Father's Authority and Government.* They had been accustomed in their Childhood to follow his Direction, and to refer their little differences to him, and when they were Men, who fitter to rule them?" (2.75). While he references an unspoken agreement, no explicit acknowledgment of this agreement is evident, as "the natural *Fathers of Families,* by an insensible change, became the *politick Monarchs of them too*" (2.76). On this account, the foundations of hereditary kingdoms are laid "according as Chance, Contrivance, or Occasions happen'd to mould them" (2.76). This narrative of the political anthropology departs from the account of voluntary, voiced agreement to a new institution of political community. More specifically, it seems to contradict Locke's claims at the conclusion of chapter 8, in the wake of the political anthropology, that nothing makes one a member of a commonwealth "but his actually entering into it by positive Engagement, and express Promise and Compact" (2.122).

Where this narrative may appear at first as a fairly innocuous tale of customary authority drawing on natural and affective ties, it comes to threaten that which Locke prizes most—governance for the good of the people. At the close of chapter 7, Locke imagines a different kind of insensible change, in which rule was passed on to sons, giving rise to "Successors of another Stamp" who showed less virtue and restraint. "[W]hen time, giving Authority, and (as some Men would perswade us) Sacredness to Customs," he writes, the people find themselves and their property at risk from the authority they once blindly trusted with "unforeseeing Innocence" (2.94). Locke attributes this shift to a rising "Ambition and Luxury" that led rulers to increase their power, with new desires of stretching their prerogative (2.111). Although Locke does not draw the connection explicitly, the economic shifts driving this thirst for power recall the earlier discussion of property in chapter 5 when he writes of an era, before the "*Invention of Money,* and the tacit Agreement of Men to put a value on it" (2.36). With money, goods are revalued, eliciting new, expanded desires, which, in turn, bring about scarcity and increased conflict. In this way, early societies come to live under expansive authority they never foresaw when they tacitly agreed to live under the rule of the father. As Ruth Grant sums up this story, the political anthropology "describes traditionalist, authoritarian, paternalistic societies."[6] In fact, the political anthropology seems to mark yet another return of Filmer's phantom fatherhood, but this time with a crucial difference: it is met with Locke's approval.

Some readers of Locke's political thought, such as Carole Pateman and Terrell Carver, see this narrative as an apparently untroubled (for Locke) admission of the paternal origins of hereditary monarchy. As such, it constitutes evidence that Locke's contractual politics is an old patriarchalism in a new guise. By holding up paternal authority alongside individual consent as legitimate, Locke reveals his notion of consent to be ultimately compatible with certain forms of patriarchal authority. To join the political anthropology to the earlier account of the origin of civil society out of the state of nature, in this way, reveals the considerably less than universal dimensions of Lockean consent as freely and expressly chosen by individuals.[7]

Other interpreters, notably Ruth Grant and Jeremy Waldron, recognize the tensions posed by the political anthropology and yet seek to reconcile it with the more familiar consensual version to retain its critical value.[8] Waldron incisively conveys the dilemma posed by the anthropological narrative. He sees a divide playing out within the text of the *Second Treatise* between the often less-than-free conditions of actual polities and the normative vision of politics by which those political arrangements can be judged. There are two origin stories for political authority in Waldron's telling, and this raises thorny issues. As he explains, "The story Locke needs (for his moral and political purposes) he cannot have (for historical reasons), and the story that is consistent and historically plausible is not one that gets him anywhere near the normative conclusions he desires."[9] In other words, the political anthropology raises the problem of critique in the *Second Treatise.*

For Waldron, the political anthropology cannot be dispensed with because it supplements Locke's abstract concepts by showing how they are to be used for judging political arrangements embedded in existing social relations and practices. He envisions a way out of the problem of critique by articulating the proper relation between the plausible history of the anthropology as the object of judgment, on the one hand, and the abstract categories by which we judge, on the other. It is the "contract story that packs the normative punch of his political philosophy" while the political anthropology is a vehicle for demonstrating the practical value of that normative purchase.[10] Through placing these normative categories like a template over the political anthropology, the plausible political history acquires meaning. While Waldron appreciates Locke's efforts at political judgment directed toward plausible political histories, he does not envision these histories offering the resources for normative purchase.

The reason Waldron does not see the political anthropology as a resource for critique is because of the model of judgment he assumes to be at work in the *Second Treatise*. He rightly sees ongoing political judgments as vital for Lockean politics. On his account, Lockean judgment requires a return to standards that, by their nature, are external to social and political practices: "Since the moral categories we have are necessary for the study of history, they cannot themselves be the product of historical study. Their basis lies in reason, or, as Dunn puts it, in the *ahistorical* arguments of natural theology."[11] Judgment, on this account, involves applying criteria to social and political conditions that do not depend on the sociohistorical contexts of particular political communities. Waldron thereby interprets the political anthropology in terms of a dichotomy that recalls Laslett's divided account of Locke, opposing the abstract as normative and transcendent against the particular as merely given.

While the political anthropology in this account distances Locke from the Kantian social contract as an idea of pure reason, the account of judgment Waldron locates in the *Second Treatise* realigns Locke with Kantian judgment as subsuming particulars under a universal determinative judgment.[12] Given what we have seen of Locke's practice of critique through the rhetorical force of particular images and idioms, we must ask whether the political anthropology might not have more to offer. For Locke, abstract and general ideas are important, particularly for moral and political judgment, but they are not so clearly distinguished from particular examples and images drawn from sensible experience. How, after all, can formless abstractions and general rules distanced from sensation and experience have the capacity to move the understanding to judgment and action? Looking at the political anthropology as a series of examples, including the tales drawn from travel literature, history, and scripture, recalls the very figures that Locke puts to such powerful critical use in the *Essay* and *First Treatise*.[13] Given the striking tales and vivid examples Locke sets to critical work in the *First Treatise*, it no longer makes sense to view the political anthropology as the "mere" matter to which normative judgment is applied.

The examples of the political anthropology demand a closer look for their contributions to the theoretical and critical content of the *Second Treatise*. Importantly, we must consider these examples both in their relation to more abstract claims and in their rhetorical effects. Kirstie McClure invites us to read these passages, both the narrative and the sometimes neglected examples, in the manner of rhetorical conventions of *fabula* and *historia*. For early modern readers, *historia* are "the deeds and events attested to by the historical record," or in Philip Sidney's words, "true stories what have bin." *Fabula* are associated universal considerations, or "pictures, what should be."[14] The pair are not neatly assimilated to fact versus fiction or abstract, normative, and universal against particular facts and images. Neither is the distinction posited a hard and fast one, as a number of early modern texts such as More's *Utopia*, Bacon's *New Atlantis*, and Harrington's *Oceana* can be seen "oscillating across that boundary."[15]

To look at the examples and narratives of the political anthropology with an eye to such rhetorical strategies and possibilities reconfigures the relation of the political anthropology to the *Second Treatise* as a whole. It is no longer a foregone conclusion that it is organized around an abstract, and thus privileged, universal under which particular cases are to be subsumed, lest the text lose its logical or normative force. On the contrary, accounts of what has been and what should be do not need to be sorted out in such a hierarchical and dichotomous manner. Instead, Locke's examples and narratives—both *historia* and *fabula* or somewhere in between them—may be read as "images aimed to engage the affects."[16] Rather than dividing the political anthropology into fact and norm, engaging such rhetorical strategies requires readers to discern meaning in a more nuanced and variegated field. The political anthropology composed of *fabula* and *historia* is not so easily differentiated from the origin stories of the state of nature and consent.

Locke's *fabula* and *historia* contribute to a broad strategy of exemplification, which requires a mode of reading that is attuned to the force of the particular as well as the universal.[17] Indeed the two for Locke, as we have seen, are interdependent. The political anthropology comes to be located within a larger narrative of judgment lost and regained, which is to say, a story of critique.

Figures of Consent

Looking first to the examples of the political anthropology, we find echoes of Locke's strategies of critique in book 1 of the *Essay* and the *First Treatise*. The examples in chapter 8 of the *Second Treatise* refute those critics who, like Filmer, argue that there never was a state of nature and polities never did arise out of consent. Locke begins his refutation with an example that is also an analogy. In denying that there was a state of nature because there is so little record, "we may as well suppose the Armies of *Salmanasser,* or *Xerxes* were never Children because we hear little of them, till they were Men, and imbodied in Armies" (2.101). Societies, like individuals, are subject to narratives of growth and change just as we saw with Locke's account of the understanding in the *Essay.* Growth and change are not necessarily the same as a story of progress, as we will see. Rather, they inaugurate an as-yet-unspecified narrative that will contrast with the immutable Fatherhood.

Locke goes on to assert that those records we do have "of the beginning of any Polities in the world ... are all either plain instances of such a beginning, or at least have manifest footsteps of it." Commonwealths, like people, are "commonly *ignorant of their own Births* and *Infancies,*" especially since political origins generally precede "Letters." Memory, for polities no less than people, leans heavily on material words. Letters that do survive—examples from history and scripture—tell us that polities begin in human agreement. Before he even finishes the paragraph, however, Locke posits the Jews as an exception because of God's direct intervention, "which favours not at all Paternal Dominion" (2.101). This conclusion, counterintuitive from a patriarchalist perspective, signals the extension of the refutation in the *First Treatise,* in which paternal dominion comes to be figured as competitive with and destructive of a worldly order compatible with God as maker. Moreover, Locke's immediate granting of an exception enacts a less dogmatic stance on political origins than Filmer's strong universalism. Locke then cites the "evident matter of fact" that Rome and Venice originated in the union of several free and equal individuals. These historical examples are complemented by Joseph Acosta's account of the absence of government in the Americas, where people remain free and equal until they agree to join into political society and choose governors and forms of government (2.102). Even those who exit existing political societies, such as those who left Sparta with Palantus, illustrate the consensual origins of polities in history. Locke leaves open the possibility that an origin in paternal authority can be found, but he is confident that history is on the side of consent, even as he declares that "at best an Argument from what has been, to what should of right be, has no great force" (2.103).

This bundle of claims and examples seems to point toward more than one conclusion about whether or not polities always originate in consent. Nonetheless, we can discern some key arguments and effects. First, Locke asserts that consent is a matter of fact if we look to history. It is not merely an abstraction but can be observed in the world. Second, it can be observed repeatedly, across time and place. These examples disprove the patriarchalist assertion of a single origin in paternal authority. However, they interestingly play out repeatedly *but not identically* over time and across the globe. So they refute not just Filmer's central claim but also his dogmatic universalism by turning a single biblical story of divine intervention into just one case among many, and an exceptional case at that. The patriarchalist account, now shown to be exception rather than rule, loses its privileged status. Locke puts before the reader vivid, likely familiar, examples of consensual origins to show, not what is universally necessary, but what is possible.

These examples do more than mark the repeated subsumption of particular instances to a concept, namely, the concept of consent. Moving through these exemplary cases of consent, we witness Locke's articulation of a notion of consent that emerges by enumerating the *matter of consent*, that is, its sensible record in the history of human action. As Locke's *Essay* posits, it is only through such particular images that a general or abstract idea of consent can be sustained and communicated with others. More precisely, the abstract notion of consent is articulated here through the analogous connections Locke draws between these diverse historical moments. Locke brings before the reader figures of consent that depict its plural and contingent forms. By finding and presenting these cases to the reader, he invents a notion of consent for which plurality and contingency are part and parcel.

Where Waldron found two origin stories in the *Second Treatise*, we now see that there are many. There is little surprise that Locke pluralizes Filmer's political origins in the *Second Treatise*, just as he did in the *First*. There are, however, some important differences. In the *First Treatise*, Locke inhabits the logic and language of patriarchalism to turn it against itself, disfiguring its organizing images and idioms. Here, in chapter 8 of the *Second Treatise*, we find Locke using the same strategies of exemplification to pluralize and decenter patriarchal claims, but the focus is now on his own privileged category of consent. Pluralizing Filmer's categories clearly targets the universalism of patriarchalism, but how can Locke's own concept maintain critical purchase when marked by the same plurality?

To put such variety of consensual origins next to the narrative of the probable origins of polities in paternal authority does not allay the concerns raised by Waldron's interpretation of the political anthropology. In fact, it accentuates the questions of judgment and critique that arise from the fact that Locke seems to see consent everywhere: how are readers, not to mention citizens, able to discern the limits of reasonable consent? At stake here is the long-standing reputation, both positive and negative, of Locke as a theorist of political critique for whom universal categories provide an external standpoint from which to judge political communities. The plurality of Lockean consent troubles this reputation, but it also yields an alternative model of critique, as we will see next.

Consent and Invention: The Case of Money

While the origins of paternal authority are found in chapters 6 through 8, the references Locke makes to an earlier era, a golden age, and a beginning, arise even earlier: in the discussion of property and money in chapter 5. One way to understand these origin stories over four chapters (rather than just three chapters) is as components of a single narrative, in which the turn from an age of innocence to one of ambition and luxury in chapter 5 provides the explanation for the rise and corruption of paternal authority in the following three chapters. Locke does *not* indicate such narrative continuity in the substance or structure of the text. There is, however, a distinct resonance among these passages in the way that Locke repeatedly hearkens back to earlier, more virtuous times. With this rhetorical gesture back to a golden age, Locke follows the manner of Ovid or Herodotus as well as a popular mode of writing in the early modern period. These backward glances establish a relation of similitude between the anthropological narrative and the examples drawn from history, scripture, and travel literature. Similarity is not the same thing as identity, however, and this distinction is crucial for understanding the meaning of these stories.

The relationship between political anthropology, tales from the Old and New World, and Locke's account of money is captured in his well-known assertion "Thus in the beginning all the World was *America*, and more so than that is now; for no such thing as *Money* was any where known" (2.49). "In the beginning" hearkens back to an indeterminate golden age, which is then tied to the present but presumably unfamiliar site, "America." Locke weaves together here otherwise temporally discontinuous indigenous people and those of a golden age. This move recalls the practices of fifteenth- and sixteenth-century writers who assimilated accounts from the New World into existing frameworks from canonical texts. Renaissance writers sought the origins of indigenous Americans and looked for them in familiar, ancient heritages. Some of these writers provided the material for Locke's examples, writers such as Joseph Acosta, who saw Amerindians as descending from the Jews, or Grotius, who envisioned a Viking background for many indigenous groups.[18]

This practice of inserting newly encountered peoples into genealogies of the old enabled early modern writers to associate them with an array of existing tropes, both positive and negative. Such relations of similitude might designate indigenous peoples as savages or cannibals, as we saw in the *First Treatise*, but as Vanita Seth explains, "It could equally be argued that the aboriginals constituted a site on which to confer legitimacy and reconfirm the authority of canonical knowledge. Does not the cannibalism of the Indians speak to a rich tapestry of sources that have testified to the existence of anthropophagy [cannibalism]? Is not the existence of a Golden Age such as that so eloquently described in the works of Hesiod, Virgil, and Ovid proved to be true in the very life of the indigenous Americans?"[19] For Seth, such narrative conventions were part of a worldview that gave way to a historically differentiated outlook of Enlightenment, represented by Locke and Rousseau.[20] Adhering too strictly to such periodization, however, obscures the fact that Locke is a threshold figure, well versed in the rhetorical conventions of the earlier age, even as he helps to inaugurate new forms. The challenge is to recognize Locke's rhetorical ingenuity in weaving together heterogeneous styles of rhetoric and philosophy. In this way, both Locke's narrative of the political anthropology and the more condensed examples from travel, scripture, and history have a common exemplary status that belongs to old and new worlds as well as old and new rhetorical styles.

We are now poised to return once more to reread the political anthropology, in chapters 5 through 8, as a mixture of rhetorical styles, of narrative and example, that present particular, illustrative images of consent, authority and its limits. The significance of this totality need not be restricted to what can be fitted into a single, linear narrative.[21] Instead, the rhetorical force of the anthropology emerges beyond the confines of a single narrative because its rhetorical conventions are repeatedly performed for various purposes and effects, just as we saw with the figure of Eve. As we will now see, Locke cycles through recurring narratives, no less than three times in the *Second Treatise*, giving readers a repetitive performance of the contingent and plural origins and fates of political authority.

In the golden age before money, we find the beginning of Locke's story of property. Through labor, individuals acquire property from the earth, given to humans in common, and it is this labor that is the source of value for such goods and land. Locke draws together examples from historical, scriptural, and travel literature to serve as matters of fact illustrating how labor is the basis for the appropriation of property, including land. In doing so, he generates an image of a former world, populated by early families seeking land for their labors; it is a world situated alongside the familiar stories of Cain and Abel, Abraham and Lot (2.38). These laboring figures are then contrasted with Americans, "who are rich in Land, and poor in all the Comforts of Life" (2.41). Indians and biblical figures here seem to share a common world, but they are not situated in the same way to the possibilities and promises of industry.

These brief examples pave the way for that earlier age when labor alone was sufficient to secure a title to property. Without the aid of positive law or impartial judges, individuals appropriated what they needed from nature, assured that there would always be enough and as good for others. Property was thus naturally bounded by the unwritten natural law prohibition on waste and spoilage. It is not that everyone obeyed the natural law as a self-executed force. Rather, humans work out the meaning of a law they have no direct access to. While each individual enjoys the right to judge and punish according to the natural law, the meaning of the natural law does not reveal itself, but rather calls upon humans to interpret it.[22] This need for careful interpretation of fragmented and obscure "texts" in early modern Epicureanism—historical, philosophical, scriptural, and even natural (as in the Book of Nature)—emphasized the importance of probable judgment from experience. Human inference and action was seen as necessary for making sense of and enacting a larger order that is only partially or indirectly available to human senses. As we have seen in the *First Treatise*, however, this state of affairs poses risks. Such order is just as easily undone by human action and the failure of judgment (1.58).

For the force of an unwritten law to depend upon human judgment and execution presumes that transgressions are evident to human understanding. As Locke writes, "[W]hat Portion a Man carved to himself, was easily seen; and it was useless as well as dishonest to carve himself too much, or take more than he needed" (2.51). From what we have seen of Locke's exegetic encounters, such interpretive projects can be anything but peaceful and conciliatory. Yet, in the early accounts of property under the natural law, Locke insists there was "no reason of quarrelling about Title, nor any doubt about the largeness of Possession it gave" (2.51). As McClure describes these natural denizens: "Theirs was a world of visceral experience, in which the administration of justice in the recognition of punishment of criminality was a broadly participatory social practice centered in the local community."[23] The enactment of the natural law was sufficiently situated within the limited realm of human experience and needs. Locke presents human judgment here as capable of enforcing an unwritten law based not on direct access to timeless truths but on the senses and reflection of limited human understandings. Locke asserts that humans have the capacity to live together lawfully and peacefully, as judging individuals, but they do so without guarantees that these conditions will always be in place.

Indeed, as Locke's story of property continues, it reveals the instability and conflict that can also arise as a consequence of human judgment and action. These simpler times are completely transformed by the introduction of money. Money emerges out of "Fancy or Agreement" (2.46).[24] This work of imagination acquires force only with its silent adoption into social practice, when "Men . . . having, by a tacit and voluntary consent, found out a way how a man may fairly possess more land than he himself can use the product of, by receiving in exchange for the overplus, Gold and Silver, which may be hoarded up without injury to any one; these metals not spoiling or decaying in the hands of the possessor" (2.50).

The invention of money brings about a sudden shift in a world without scarcity to a world of unlimited human appropriation. It is an interruption and redirection in social practices that could not have happened without "the *Invention of Money*, and the tacit Agreement of Men to put a value on it, introduced (by Consent) larger Possessions, and a Right to them" (2.36). Money creates the possibility of accumulation for its own sake by giving durability to goods where nature alone does not. Thus, the natural limitation on property—spoilage—is circumvented. Convention and invention come together to extend the lifespan of both nature and human labor (2.46, 50). Tacit consent to a novel practice catapults societies into a different social order that brings with it a new economy, a new psychology, and a new temporality.

With human judgment enacting both natural and conventional measures of value, societies come to be propelled by new forces. The marginal advantages accorded to the rational and industrious become far greater, and thus, for Locke, humans tacitly agree to a "disproportionate and unequal Possession of the Earth" (2.50). Land becomes scarce and property disputes more frequent. The conditions resemble that of the state of war or at least for inconveniences serious enough to drive people to form civil societies (2.123). The natural limits to property are not eliminated, but they have come to be felt far less immediately. There is, in other words, a loss of the experiential basis of judgment of the simple days before money. Tacit consent to money transforms the effect—we might even say the force—of the natural law.

The origin story of money demonstrates the contingent nature of consent and reasonable judgment in the political anthropology. The inventors of money may have envisioned the instrumental advantages of establishing this conventional measure of value and appropriation, but they are also transformed by their invention. They become subject to the unintended consequences of their own actions. The broader horizons opened up by money bring with them new desires: the time before money was also the time "before the desire of having more than Men needed" (2.37). With this new system of social valuation, desires are animated by the new possibility of unlimited accumulation of property. Money is at once a product of imagination and a practice that spurs on human imaginations in novel directions. Transforming the relationship between humans, the material world, and natural law, money introduces a contingency in the temporality of social life in marked contrast to the eternal necessity of Filmer's timeless universals. That contingency extends to the capacity of humans to judge well based on their limited understanding, as evidenced in the loss of the *sensible* limits of accumulation.

Chapter 5 of the *Second Treatise* offers not just a story of invention and consent but also one of reasonable judgment. Locke's vision of labor giving title to property depends upon the faculty of judgment for community self-regulations according to an unwritten law. When that form of judgment comes to be transformed by human activity of a different sort, we see that the conditions of such visceral, experience-based judgment may not always be guaranteed. Judgment and activity give practical form and force to the law of nature and then by virtue of further judgments and actions, the difficulties of a more covetous and less abundant world are unleashed. While Locke's designation of tacit consent invites readers to see these actions as reasonable, his account also illustrates how social relations entered into voluntarily and reasonably may yield insecure and unfreeing consequences. When that happens, Locke does not seek to retract such practices or to caution against future innovation. Rather, he looks forward to new judgments and actions.

As judgment under natural law gives way to a crisis elicited by money's transformation of the conditions of judgment, the stage is set for the rise of civil society and the restoration of judgment. The call to judgment rings throughout the *Second Treatise*, most famously in the closing chapters, in which Locke declares that "[t]he People shall be Judge" (2.240). The form of judgment highlighted in the origin of money is one that is practically oriented and based in experience. As Douglas Casson writes, "The faculty of judgment based on visible and tangible experience is the animating force of our political life."[25] Yet that same tale recounts the loss of conditions under which such judgment could secure peace and security. Human action, Locke shows us, is transformative, not only of material conditions, but also of human relations and subjectivities. In other words, the subjects and the community who judge do not stand outside the social forces they enact. The creation of civil society is presented as the political solution to this crisis in judgment. When we turn back to the origins of paternal authority, however, we find that this portrayal of the transformative effects of social practices on experiential judgment generates a problem of political critique that is not confined to a prepolitical past.

Recollecting Fathers and Kings: Repetition and Critique

The invention of money prefigures Locke's several passages on the origins of political authority in inherited monarchies. In the chapters that follow, Locke repeatedly touches back to political origins in tacit agreement(s) between familial relations rather than express consent. These origins conform in many ways to the broad contours of the Filmerian account. Locke does not shy from this counter-narrative but rather seeks to bring it into the fold of contingent consent. It is a tall order, however, to persuade those who, following Filmer, would see their current political conditions as a continuation of a timeless patriarchal order to believe that such arrangements were the contingent outcome of consensual arrangements. Locke's continual return to the paternal origins of government speaks to this question of experience and critique. Rather than posing a challenge to the abstract standards of the *Second Treatise*, the political anthropology should be seen as an alternative rendering of this familiar tale. Casson calls it an "alternative history" that is "more factual, more readily observable, and more obviously compatible with the available evidence," and thus capable of eliciting judgments of probability that resist the patriarchalist narrative.[26] Locke does indeed look to particular examples to displace Filmer's seemingly timeless and universal rule of father-kings. The crisis of judgment elicited by money, however, reveals that this project is significantly more complicated than the marshaling of these examples as readily observable facts suggests.

The notion that Lockean judgment proceeds from experience is an important one, but it is also complicated. In emphasizing the material conditions of this judgment, we cannot ignore the play of the visible and invisible, the sensible and the insensible, the consent and the silence, that drive Locke's stories of judgment and loss. Nor should we fall back on the dichotomy by which claims of experience mark the exclusion of language, particularly rhetoric. As we have seen, humans enact and give force to an *unwritten* law of nature by virtue of their visceral experience. That experiential quality of needs and transgressions comes to be *insensible* in the wake of human action in the form of an agreement made in *silence*. Locke's story of judgment based on observable facts is never free of the unobservable and insensible. Nor is the observable immune to obfuscation by human innovation and its unintended consequences.

The interplay of sensible and insensible in chapter 5 signals that Locke's claim to experience requires more than the force of facts to sustain critique. He needs a new relation to the past. That project requires the finding of new similarities or

relations amid difference, requiring invention. Locke's narratives of paternal authority perform an inventive practice of seeing the past anew that is not possible without rhetoric. More specifically, that project is located in Locke's repeated
returns—no less than three times—to recount the origins of government in paternal authority, using these stories to speak to familiar (but seemingly patriarchal)
experience and to show that experience in a new light. To consider such accounts
only as facts does not help us to recognize the multifaceted way that Locke uses
these narratives to generate new relations of similarity between the past and a
future that might be otherwise. As we will see, just as in the story of the rise of
money, the actors in these tales also exhibit the capacity for inventive activity that
is essential to understanding the limits and promises of human judgment as a
source of political authority as well as critique.

Locke has surprisingly little difficulty admitting the ease with which fathers
must have become kings in the first ages: "[Y]et 'tis obvious to conceive how easie it
was in the first Ages of the World, and in places still, where the thinness of People
gives Families leave to separate into unpossessed Quarters . . . for the *Father of the
Family* to become the Prince of it" (2.74). For Laslett, Locke's admission that early
rulers were often fathers marks a concession to patriarchalism that shows "some
signs that [Locke] recognized the limitations of his own intellectualistic rationalism."[27] Laslett is right to see Locke beyond the limits of rationalism in these
passages, but not because they represent a concession to patriarchalism.
Instead Locke recounts a tale of father-kings that emphasizes human workmanship and contingency, to generate an entirely different image of political
fatherhood. Where Filmer naturalizes relations of subjection, Locke shows us
how they might have arisen as the effect of human action and inaction, invention
and convention.

In Locke's first engagement with paternal authority over adults in chapter 6, he
argues that it comes not from the dictates of God or nature but from the suspension of natural rights among grown children: by "permitting the *Father* to exercise
alone in his Family that executive Power of the Law of Nature, which every Free-
man naturally hath, and by that permission resigning up to him a Monarchical
Power, whilst they remained in it. But that was not by *Paternal Right*, but only by
the Consent of his Children." The rule of the father arises as a shared practice
enacted by his grown children through unspoken, that is, enacted but not voiced
agreement. Locke calls this tacit agreement "almost natural" and "scarce avoidable"
(2.75). This practice does not follow from the application of natural law but from
the *drawing of an analogy* to the law of nature. That analogy is the result of human

activity. Such early peoples reproduce familiar relations of authority in new circumstances. What may seem like the "mere" repetition of nature is productive of political innovation. By making visible an otherwise hidden form of consent, Locke finds both consent and invention, enacted by adult sons and daughters, in what otherwise appears as subjection and necessity.

As with the rise of money, Locke uses tacit consent to render visible what he sees as an otherwise unannounced human action. In doing so, he opens up the question of why such tacit consent would be given. He suggests reasons of affection, a tenderness and care shown in the past by such fathers as well as children who have grown accustomed to his authority (2.75). Passions and habit form the basis for such authority, which comes into being through "an insensible change" (2.76). What is observable here is not consent, or even the question of who should hold authority. Rather, judgments proceed here from affective and customary attachments that have rendered a change in authority insensible. These judgments may well be based in experience, but experience here is not simply facts but a passionate and customary relation to those facts.

That these early people made these choices does not make them binding on those who come after, however. In the very next chapter, Locke reasserts his claims of the *First Treatise* by distinguishing paternal and political authority. At the close of chapter 7, he returns to a time "at first" in which perhaps "some one good and excellent Man . . . had this Deference paid to his Goodness and Vertue, as to a kind of Natural Authority . . . by a tacit consent" (2.94). The key points are reiterated from the earlier account of paternal authority in chapter 6—tacit consent, a worthy single leader, a seemingly natural authority—though fathers are neither specifically mentioned nor excluded. In chapter 7, however, this version continues further to recount a darker turn of events to those successors of another stamp. Here, as well, Locke provides the reason for the change: "time, giving Authority, and (as some Men would perswade us) Sacredness to Customs, which the negligent, and unforeseeing Innocence of the first Ages began" (2.94). Not only do early rulers take on authority through insensible change but the notion that they and their successors should continue in power, too, carries on without notice. With this second iteration of the rise of one man to authority through tacit consent, a new, expanded perspective on those people of the first ages emerges. Previously driven by familiarity and affection, they now appear negligent and unforeseeing. Putting these two accounts of the early days into relationship shows forward movement in time, but it does not necessarily forward one narrative. Locke shows the early adult sons and daughters in a new and less flattering light that expands upon, without replacing, the earlier version. Their judgment based in experience appears first as reasonable and is then subsequently shown to become woefully inadequate. The text now offers two perspectives on the same past. These dual perspectives recall the depiction of judgment regarding property in the early ages and after the rise of money.

In chapter 8, we find the third, and most extended, set of passages in which Locke revisits the early days of paternal authority. In chapter 8 alone, there are three iterations of the early days when fathers were kings, broken up by the examples from history, scripture, and travel accounts discussed above. Each one, then, is a new turn back, yielding both repetition and the difference that enables ever more plural perspectives and deeper critical understanding. In sections 105–8, Locke picks up the vocabulary we now recognize from previous iterations of the rise of paternal authority. In the beginning, before ambitions grew, fathers rose to "Preheminency" because of the care and affection they had shown to their (now grown) sons and daughters (2.106). It was the arrangement that "by experience they had found both easie and safe." Locke reiterates that such paternal authority was "most obvious and simple" (2.107). In this version, he reflects more deeply, however. Such a father-king "was fittest to be trusted; Paternal affection secured their Property, and Interest under his Care, and the Custom of obeying him, in their Childhood, made it easier to submit to him, rather than any other" (2.105). He speaks of how these early peoples were free of concerns about trespasses on property and injustice. In this way, Locke draws more explicit ties to the ends that will shape his vision of political authority: the protection of property and the security and good of the people. He then presses his own assessment of such political conditions further, pronouncing paternal authority "best suited to their present State and Condition" (2.107). This is a stronger claim affirming paternal authority, not just as one possibility, but as the preferable one above others. His claims proceeds, however, from the "State and Condition" in which these people are situated. Those conditions are circumscribed by the changes Locke describes over the repeated cycles of his account of paternal authority. It is only in this third iteration that readers are positioned to view these conditions from the plurality of perspectives that allow Locke to strongly, yet conditionally, endorse the very form of rule he otherwise opposes.

In sections 110–12, the tale replays yet again of a family growing up into a commonwealth. Locke emphasizes the contingency and plurality of this political origin. In some cases, a single family became a political community, while in other cases it was the union of several families, brought together by "Chance, Neighbourhood, or Business" (2.110), not unlike the contingent material conditions that inaugurated the *Essay*. The same reasonable judgment applies here, whereby rule is placed in the hands of one trusted man for reasons of "the publick Good and Safety" (2.110), in an era free of the later vices of ambition and luxury (2.111). A variety of political situations, all resulting from the same mode of reasoning from experience, now comes before the reader. An important shift has occurred here. This exploration of early political societies begins in response to the sense that kings had always been, and should therefore always be, father figures, and vice versa. He reworks the account of father-kings such that they come from reasoned judgment based on experience, that is, situated contingently rather than universally. Father-kings thereby come to appear as one among a variety of political arrangements settled upon reasonably but contingently by humans. These shifting figures of paternal authority culminate in the striking image of "nursing Fathers tender and carefull of the publick weale" (2.110) where they are essential for the survival of polities but only in a temporary condition that is subordinated to the good of the people. Far from the monstrous and profligate images projected in the *First Treatise*, the Fatherhood is refigured into a sort of political mother, a hybrid figure drawing together the temporary and circumscribed authority of Eve with the political standing reserved for men.

We find Locke, rather than recounting a single anthropological narrative, incrementally introducing and revising the story of how fathers came to be kings. With each iteration, the reader's view is expanded to encompass different perspectives on this seemingly familiar past. As readers, we are repeatedly reminded of the experiential judgment underlying tacit consent to all forms of government (even that of father-kings) as well as the power of passions and habit in sustaining that authority. Central to this transformative retelling is the project of *making visible* that which was insensible to those who enacted it: tacit consent and unpredictable social and political change. While Locke insists on the reasonableness of the judgment of those who picked caring fathers to rule for the public good, it is only with the explanation of tacit consent and insensible change that readers are led to judge "how probable it is, that People that were naturally free, and by their own consent ... should generally put the *Rule into one Man's hands*" (2.112). Here we see most clearly that Locke not only is concerned to defend the judgment of early peoples but also is also focused on a larger project of cultivating the judgment of his readers. It is this cultivation of judgment by example that requires the continued repetition and transformation of the origin stories of paternal authority.

Finally, in section 115, Locke returns a last time to the beginning ages to show that "there are no Examples so frequent in History, both Sacred and Prophane, as those of Men withdrawing themselves, and their Obedience, from the Jurisdiction they were born under, and the Family or Community they were bred up in, and *setting up new Governments* in other places, from whence sprang all that number of petty Common-wealths in the beginning of Ages." As Locke looks to an earlier era for support, he effects a sharp reversal of what has so far been found in this distant past. Where the early ages initially seemed to affirm the prevalence, even desirability, of paternal authority under certain conditions, now this bygone age evidences an all-too-familiar need to break with authority. That a monarch holds authority over one polity among others—that there is no ruler on earth with a universally valid claim to authority—testifies to the improbable claims of patriarchalism. In other words, the multiplicity of polities, inclusive even of those that proclaim their king as divinely appointed father of the nation, come to serve as evidence of the consensual nature of politics.

That relation to the past also serves as a launching pad for a different future. The story of paternal authority as one of judgment and consent, Locke argues, proves that one "*cannot* by any *Compact* whatsoever, bind *his Children* or Posterity" (2.116). Looking backward, the problem that Locke identifies is not the absence of consent. Rather, it is inattention to the judgments and actions undertaken to maintain authority, sometimes tacitly. The problem surrounding consent is that it is forgotten and neglected: "[p]eople take no notice of it, and thinking it not done at all, or not necessary, conclude they are naturally Subjects as they are Men" (2.117). Locke calls readers back to attention but not to what was always obvious. Rather, he calls their attention to what he has inventively brought before their sight: the matter of consent.

Locke takes a fairly simple fact—the plurality of political communities—to sustain a conclusion that is far from obvious: the freedom to separate from family and government to establish a new political society. We should not be lulled into accepting as self-evident arguments such as these that Locke and his heirs have made to seem almost natural to late modern citizens of liberal democratic polities. These claims come to seem natural because of their repetition across time and place. We too, as late modern readers, become accustomed to them and their rhetorical conventions such that we come to see our political practices through these idioms. For Locke's first readers, those conventions and idioms were not already oriented toward consent, though consent was not a new idea.[28] It is by coming on the heels of these successive narratives of father-kings, withdrawal, and refounding, though, that Locke's claims in this final turn to the early ages come to seem less surprising. Nonetheless, we should not ignore how they trumpet what could easily be viewed as frequent rebellion and sinful disobedience.

The recurring narratives that compose the political anthropology reveal relations of similarity based on consent and judgment from experience where none were apparent. In this way, Locke makes visible a past that would not necessarily be evident to those who lived it, or those who followed. He invites readers to see things from the perspective of these early peoples, to understand why it is that they would find it reasonable to appoint fathers as kings. He thus affirms their reasonable judgment and enables readers to do the same by providing a probable reasoning for their actions. Yet these exemplary tales do not illustrate an unfolding freedom and security from this reinvented past. On the contrary, these figures of consent and tales of judgment meet unhappy fates, victims of unintended consequences and unscrupulous successors. This hardly seems a ringing endorsement of the judgment of the people. Yet Locke expresses his faith in this very judgment: "But whatever Flatterers may talk to amuze Peoples Understandings, it hinders not Men, from Feeling: and when they perceive that any Man, in what Station soever, is out of Bounds of the Civil Society . . . and that they have no Appeal on Earth against any harm they may receive from him, they are apt to think themselves in the state of Nature . . . and to take care as soon as they can, to have that *Safety and Security in Civil Society*" (2.94). Locke makes a strong appeal here to visceral experience, which is to call on the disruptive quality of experience as the grounds for critique of authority. Yet, as we have seen, custom and habit can lead to inattention and naive obedience. The challenge that emerges from Locke's political anthropology is that enduring practices breed attachment and people become blind to changes around them: the less virtuous leaders, expanded desires, and increasing social conflict. What once seemed like a reasonable set of judgments based on experience comes to be a failure to recognize what is new in the world. It is a failure to see in new ways, to envision new categories of understanding, as well as a failure to recall the human judgment and inventive activity that went into producing conditions that come to seem "almost natural" and "scarce avoidable." Moreover, it is a failure to recognize the potential novelty that ensues whenever we act. What happens when the contingent has come to seem like the given without notice? What is the source of social and political change when the contingent comes to seem as though it is the given insensibly, without a palpable feeling of loss? What happens when the people have forgotten their capacity to judge, and thus their freedom?

Critique Between Past and Future

The solution to the problems of authority recounted in the political anthropology is a new social compact, which depends on the people's judgment of their condition of subjection. The classic account of express consent in the state of nature does not offer a solution, however, to the problem of political judgment highlighted by the political anthropology. The social contract as an external framework, in particular, offers no account of how judgment and political sensibilities, once dulled and acclimated to the status quo, can be reawakened. Such accounts, rather, posit a radical break with all social and political relations that have come before. To envision a radical break in this way may seem to promise freedom, but it comes at the cost of a willful forgetting of history and particularity that has sustained defenses of imperial subjugation, expropriation of indigenous lands, and domination in the private realm.[29] Whether we adopt a critical or admiring stance toward such a break, it cannot solve that problem of judgment because it presupposes a mode of rationality that is challenged by the political anthropology. This is not the only way to understand the relationship between the social contract and political anthropology or consent and history, however.

It is often noted that Locke, unlike so many of his contemporaries, did not turn back to history in the mode of the ancient constitution in order to defend limited monarchical authority.[30] To break with the ancient constitution tradition, however, is not necessarily to break with the past as such. If we look to Locke's political anthropology as a resource for reframing and reanimating judgment—in other words, as the basis for political critique—we find that Locke draws upon a central theme driving so many of his contemporaries in their appeals to the ancient constitution: immemorial custom.[31] Locke engages in a mode of turning back to forgotten customary practices, though he does not do so to locate an authoritative precedent in the past.[32] The customary practices as well as eruptions of novelty recall a past that Locke does not associate, strictly speaking, with historical precedent, since governments, like people, are generally ignorant of their births (2.110). At the same time, he recounts the political anthropology to recall readers back to an ongoing practice of contingent judgment. Rather than trying to preserve an ancient precedent or return to it, Locke conveys the absence of a guaranteed framework for social and political practices. This absence is the condition of an alternative relation to the past for the readers of the Second Treatise.

The political anthropology, composed of examples from history, scripture, travel literature, and recurring narratives, invites readers into such a new relation. It is a call made through familiar images used as exemplars viewed from a plurality of perspectives. In Casson's account, Locke creates an alternate history from matters of fact that offers a new vocabulary of judgment.[33] Launching a new vocabulary, however, requires more than matters of fact. The political anthropology includes that recounting of facts, but it needs to do more than this. Readers are invited to relate to this past, to recognize the reasonable, though limited, record of human judgment and action. Recognizing the importance of narrative to such a historical account, Joshua Foa Dienstag calls attention to the way that this history can also be seen as a memory.[34] Yet narrative, on his account, remains in the service of philosophical principles: "Rather than history providing evidence for a theory, it is the philosophy that supplies the vocabulary for a narrative."[35] To speak of the creation of new vocabularies issuing from new memories and histories reaches beyond what philosophical principles can produce. It is the work of generating meaning and of affective (re)orientations. It is the work of rhetoric that is the condition for judgment beyond existing opinions, or in other words, the condition of critique.

The problem of subjection to overreaching authority that emerges in the political anthropology, as we have noted, is the story of human fallibility: failures of perception, of imagination, and of memory. Toward the close of the *Second Treatise*, Locke offers a hope that "those to come, redeem'd from the Impositions of those *Egyptian* Under-Taskmasters, will abhor the Memory of such servile Flatterers, who whilst it seem'd to serve their turn, resolv'd all Government into absolute Tyranny, and would have all Men born to, what their mean Souls fitted them for, Slavery" (2.239). Locke appeals to memory here but not to the living memory of any particular people. Rather, the memory that he hopes for is located in the future. It is the memory of those to come who will think back on the present as a time of slavery. It is, in other words, a memory yet to come.

To speak of a memory yet to come is to recognize the important work of memory-building for political critique, specifically to serve as the grounds of judgment for resistance and the possibility of consenting to new arrangements. Yet the memory that Locke hopes for does not follow necessarily from historical events. The past must be recalled and put into relation with a future that could be otherwise. In the *Second Treatise*, that future is inaugurated by the social contract. By offering his reimagined account of social and political experience, Locke lays the groundwork for this classic device of political critique, but this work goes beyond a new set of abstract political concepts. His project includes that conceptual work, but it proceeds by putting before his readers' sight images of freedom, judgment, and security as well as their loss. By drawing from an account of political origins that is not radically new, but reworks ideas familiar from patriarchalist accounts, Locke invites his readers to imagine themselves in a different story of political authority. That story begins with contingent consent, requires ongoing probable judgment, but then culminates in loss. This Epicurean materialist tale recalls us to the uncertainty and crises that condition Locke's critique throughout the *Essay* and *First Treatise*. Indeed, he solicits the passions of his readers to generate a new perspective on their experience. He seeks to generate that sense of uneasiness that he identifies as the impetus for entering into a new social compact. To spur the passions as well as judgment and will, in this way, requires effective and inventive speech.

That effective and inventive speech is found in the political anthropology, which now appears far from incidental to or obstructive of a new social compact but, rather, is the condition of its possibility. The memories offered up by the political anthropology serve as the material grounds of judgment from which Locke legitimates the possibility of resistance. Those memories—in the plural— are produced through exemplary images juxtaposing a present enslavement with a past natural freedom and a hypothetical future liberation. The political anthropology resituates readers in an alternative chronology. What once seemed old, if not timeless, is new: "*Jure Divino*, which we never heard of among Mankind, till it was revealed to us by the Divinity of this last Age" (2.112). By contrast, consent and its revocation are made familiar as established social practices through a recurring textual practice: the writing and rewriting of consent. The abstract idea of social contract comes to appear reasonable and plausible because, Locke shows readers, we have always instituted political authority through consent; we have always judged from experience; and we have always held the capacity to begin social and political practices anew, even if we sometimes forget that we can.

CONCLUSION

Critical Temporalities

Locke challenges authoritative claims to truth and political authority with an appeal to experience that, we now see, encompasses sensory, reflective, passionate, and rhetorical forces. He deploys these forces within a relationship established between reader and author, where contingency is brought to the foreground in politics as well as philosophy. His practice of critique in both the *Essay* and the *Two Treatises* demonstrates the vital role of imaginative language in preparing the grounds for probable judgment based in experience. Seen as a model for readers, this critical work of rhetoric challenges several familiar versions of Locke's thought. His creative deployment of particular examples and their pluralizing effects stands in contrast to the notion of the social contract as an external framework for political judgment. Locke's diverse feminine and masculine figures cannot be contained in a simple patriarchal organization of empowered male citizens and silenced wives and mothers. The artful and even cunning disfiguring and refiguring of authority stubbornly refuses Locke's image as the hard-nosed empiricist hostile to aesthetic dimensions of experience. Instead, the texts considered here reveal a mode of critique that inhabits particular social, historical, and political images and idioms to reinvent experience as the grounds from which to envision other possibilities and futures.

He reveals for his readers the conditions of production of authority in mental and social life, recounting the powerful work of ideas, imagination, and words in cementing associations and phantoms that unnecessarily bind individuals and communities. Yet he also demonstrates how figure, style, and invention are indispensable for generating meaning from the broken fragments through which we gain limited knowledge of the natural world, of history, and of sacred texts, in other words, the importance of rhetoric in reconstructing knowledge and normative frameworks. The work of rhetoric in Locke's defense and performance of judgment does not indicate a retreat from his claim to experience. Rather, it requires that we recognize that as sensing and sensible creatures, humans may need their attention and their passions oriented in new ways, to recognize that there may be other ways of seeing and feeling. This work of making visible, or audible, or palpable, for others calls out for a materialist conception of language. Language need not be a retreat from materialism but rather can be an extension of it. Material words, visible and audible, play on the mind, passions, and body. They are indeed one way that our social and political world is registered materially in and on us. We are not simply blank slates, however. As Locke shows, we can author and use material words to draw on experience and generate meaning for others. In this way, the Lockean subject shares in the capacity, once the province of the orator, to shape the conditions of judgment. Now, however, it is a capacity that is limited insofar as no one has a special claim to its use over others.

As we have discovered in two of Locke's most influential works, the rhetorically inventive use of material words is an indispensable resource for enacting critique that is situated in experience of the natural, social, and political world. This insight invites us to reconsider some of the legacies associated with Locke's thought. In particular, we are left with the rather strange conclusion that the very images of femininity and foreignness that have raised Locke's text up for feminist and postcolonial criticism may be among the richest resources for his account of philosophical and political critique. These figures, which I have argued are fundamental to his critique of timeless universal claims, have much more familiarly been taken as evidence of his own false universalism. If these figures are a site in which to discern a more robust legacy of Locke's thought for political critique, beyond empiricism and liberalism, does this new horizon of possibility also leave a remainder? The work of rhetoric, as Locke tells us, can obscure as well as render sensible. How then do we come to understand the critical reception of these feminine and foreign figures in light of Locke's rhetorical debts and claim to experience?

There are political stakes in the creation of new political temporalities, as we saw in the preceding chapter. To be more precise, there are further political questions raised by Locke's presentation of images of new and old worlds, particularly when they are located in a past that is left behind with a new social compact. This is the contention made by feminist and postcolonial critics of Locke, and of contractarianism more generally, who contend that the notion of the social contract depends covertly upon a sexual and a racial contract. These political stakes are no less part of Locke's legacy than his liberalism or empiricism. If we have arrived at a new understanding of Locke's social contract, such that it proceeds on the basis of a material account of social and political pasts that are generated through imaginative language as well as matters of fact, do we come to understand Locke's sexual contract and racial contract differently as well?

In Carole Pateman's classic formulation of the sexual contract, Locke presents marriage and family as part of the natural condition, situating women as naturally subject to the authority of fathers and husbands and excluded from full political membership.[1] As we saw in chapter 4, Locke naturalizes women's inferiority and does little to suggest that women should necessarily wield political authority (though he acknowledges that they can). Giving due attention to his feminine figures, however, reveals a more complicated picture beyond the polarized logic opposing femininity in its varied incarnations to the political man of reason. By taking up Adam as iconic political father and husband, Locke relies upon Eve as the figure that breaks the patriarchalist logic. The voice of reasoned political critique in the *First Treatise* depends on the malleability of feminine and masculine figures alike rather than a fixed ascription of meaning to women as subordinate creatures. By recognizing the rhetorical nature of Locke's feminine figures, we also discover the means by which such images—conventional and ultimately unfreeing—can be subverted and transformed. It is not by ignoring or stripping away Locke's comments on naturally inferior wives or his silence on women in the public realm in pursuit of seemingly more universal abstractions. Rather, Lockean critique, we now see, invites late modern readers to emphasize and even amplify the plural and unruly role of these feminine figures in order to disrupt their familiar, patriarchal significance.

Having already explored at some length Locke's creative and critical dependence on his various feminine figures in the *First Treatise*, we are now poised to consider the meaning of another significant image recurring in Locke's political

and philosophical writing, that of the foreigner and more specifically the indigenous inhabitant of the Americas. To recall, we have encountered examples of such
New World natives in each of the past three chapters in the form of Peruvian
cannibals in the *Essay* and the *First Treatise* and as the Indians of America in the
Second Treatise. In the *Essay*, cannibalism, in narratives including but not limited
to Garcilaso de la Vega's account of Peru, serves as a stubborn refutation of innate
ideas. New World cultural practices, with cannibalism as the most dramatic, stand
as exceptions to any universal moral or legal standard. In the *First Treatise*, Locke
returns to Garcilaso's account again, recounting from it at greater length and more
vividly. Once more, this account presents an example that denies even the most
minimal commonalities across time and space. This time, however, the example is
made more threatening for the length and detail of the passage that Locke reproduces in his own pages. These New World cannibals are made to represent the
extremes of irrationality and unchecked imagination. These encounters press us
to consider now how the "racial contract" in Locke's work as identified by Charles
Mills can be engaged in new ways given the rhetorical and experiential dimensions of Lockean critique.

Like Pateman, Mills sees the social contract as premised on relations of naturalized domination, in which the bodies, labor, and land of nonwhite subjects—
enslaved, colonized, and indigenous populations—are available for forcible
possession by others, those parties to the traditional, white and European, social
contract.[2] The numerous examples from the New World and Old that we have
explored so far invite us to consider if the picture might be more complex. While
both the *Essay* and the *Second Treatise* can be seen as offering a racialized anthropology that underwrites Lockean critique, they do not necessarily operate consis-
tently across texts. As Daniel Carey suggests, "There are grounds for seeing Locke
as offering two different anthropologies in his work."[3] So we must look more carefully at the different ways that Locke figures his "Indian" and how it contributes to
his reinvention of political authority in the past, present, and future. The *Essay*
draws from the rhetorical conventions of travel literature to assert a plurality that
refutes the universalism of innatists. The *First Treatise* draws from some of the
very same sources to refute the universalism of patriarchalists. Locke's Indian in
the *Second Treatise*, however, functions differently. More closely approximating
Locke's wives and mothers, the Indian in this text appears as a feature of the state
of nature but fades from view with the new foundation and temporality of political society. Where the sexual contract describes the condition of wives and mothers as relegated to the private realm, Locke's Indian too seems fixed in the past,

excluded from contractual futures.[4] Recalling the *Second Treatise*, "in the beginning" is described as a condition much like that of America, where its inhabitants occupy a world without money, where labor gives title to property. On the one hand, this example speaks of a rationality that is different from that of societies with more complex political and economic arrangements but a rationality that is no less appropriate to its situation. On the other hand, Locke holds up indigenous peoples in the Americas as examples of those who have not improved upon the land, giving them an impoverished existence that could be transformed by more industrious actors (2.37–43). Locke famously ties industry to rationality, further suggesting that the Indian lacks not only the activity but also the reason required for a fully developed economic and political system. There is a dual character to these Amerindian figures who, in Vanita Seth's formulation, "are at once irrational and at other times constitute still-life portraits of pre-political, rational individuals."[5]

Variously presented as reasonable judges of contingent authority and as idle occupiers of land, these foreign figures constitute vivid images of human faculties as well as the failure to cultivate them. It is not enough, however, to say that Locke simply offers a range of representations, both positive and negative, of these New World inhabitants. That they are depicted as rational even as they are positioned in distinction to members of civil society means that the *Second Treatise* depicts more than one mode of rationality. Does the social contract provide a place for alternative rationalities or are they a casualty of a single authoritative political and epistemological order? The answer to this question depends upon how we understand Locke's figuring of the "Indian" in relation to the establishment of political authority. Seth provides one way of reading Locke's Indian as ultimately an amalgam of these examples of differing significance as well as of all the narratives of the political anthropology, constituting a single prepolitical figure, "reflective of a *particular* way of being in the world, but irrational—a refusal to become a *universal* individuated being."[6] Consolidated as that which is excluded by the abstract individualism of the contracting subject, this foreign figure is situated as the remainder of a masterful rationality ascribed to Locke. One strength of this interpretation is that it emphasizes the central importance of the Indian to Locke's articulation of the rationality required for politics, even if it is as remainder to it.

This reading, however, acknowledges the plurality of Locke's foreign figures only to discard this insight for a univocal political argument. On the one hand, that Locke offers a variety of foreign figures does not mean that they are representative of the diverse matters of fact about actual people and societies that were available to Locke and his contemporaries about indigenous peoples.[7] On the other hand, the plurality of these tropes is still theoretically significant. As tropes of particularity that (sometimes) illustrate the contingency of judgment and of political authority, they raise a key question about whether they stand in uniform opposition to a univocal political subject identified with detached rationality. More specifically, the question is whether Locke's Indian stands as a remainder to the social contract once we consider the repetitions and disruptions of the political anthropology as an integral part of the social contract tale.

The alternative memory that begins with father-kings and culminates in conditional judgment and consent as a familiar practice, at first glance, carries two possible implications. First, the social contract seems to depend on a past given vivid form through the depiction of New World inhabitants, who are then excluded from a future that could be otherwise. Alternatively, a future freed of such exclusionary conditions would seem to require turning a blind eye to this reconstructed memory and its affective force. To speak not just of a memory, but of a memory yet to come, as Locke does, generates a third possibility, however. Recall the way that Locke puts exemplary figures before his readers and invites them to look from multiple perspectives. This is why it is so important to recognize the recurring cycles of narrative in the political anthropology. The stopping and starting over of these narratives of a reinvented past allows readers to see how reasonable judgments and institutions of authority are transformed by context, affective attachment, and human action as well as inaction. They depict how political judgments are not guaranteed through time and may come to appear misguided in retrospect. Moreover, Locke presents these early events in a way that invites approval as well as disapproval. Their actions made sense, *at one time*. That they no longer preserve a natural freedom does not mean that such a past should be forgotten. Nor do such past actions irrevocably bind a people to their consequences. Locke's reasoned freedom requires the capacity and the will to begin again, when needed. As we now see, it also requires an understanding of the past as productive of a future freedom and such an understanding may require rhetorical invention.

Inheriting the past as recounted through the exemplars and multiple narratives of the political anthropology resituates readers in a new relation to the past and to the future. The discontinuity of these narratives allows for both positive and negative identification with the past. As readers of the *Second Treatise*, we are invited to recognize ourselves too as denizens of a past. Readers may now see themselves as the subjects of a memory yet to come, just as they look back on the past with successive waves of recollection, some more favorable than others. We could even say that the continual starting over of the narratives of the political anthropology performs the openness to critical revision of human judgment and political authority that Locke advocates. This is one more way that his Epicurean materialist style performs the method he theorizes. By inheriting the contingent judgment of early peoples—whether foreign, biblical, or classical—we as readers also become predecessors of those who continue to judge. These future judges might be others or they may be future versions of ourselves, though separated by time and perhaps place. Either way, they will judge both in relation to and across context, generating the possibility that reasonable judgments and actions will come to appear unreasonable as social and political conditions change.

By inviting readers to look back on the present moment in just the way Locke looks back on the political anthropology, the political anthropology offers an analogy that transforms the situation of the reader. The figure of the Indian is necessary for Locke's placement of the reader as judging political subject: the reader must judge his or her own political situation after the manner of Locke's narration of this political past. Just as the Fatherhood was transformed by its juxtaposition to various iterations of iconic mothers, so the reader is recast with each new perspective on the denizens of a political past. If Locke's Indian exemplifies a mode of reasoning and acting that is confined to the past, the contracting subject may turn out to have more in common with these foreigners than expected. The "foreigner" may not be so strange, after all; or, to put it differently, readers may be rendered unfamiliar to themselves. That is not to say that either lacks rationality, but that both may look back and come to reconsider their reasonable judgments of the past. They may both come to relate to their own past in new ways, particularly as that past comes to be told as part of narratives that continually break and restart. For Locke's Indian as for the free subject rationality is always limited and mitigated by its contingent situation.

Contesting the Empire of Uniformity

In *Strange Multiplicity*, James Tully calls for an understanding of political freedom that moves beyond a mutually exclusive relation between critical freedom and adherence to custom. He contends that a critical freedom attuned to the irreducible diversity of human life requires that we reassess and reinvent the legacy of modern constitutionalism and the articulations of rights, reason, and equality that it encompasses. He concludes that "it is not too extravagant to suggest . . . that the failure to recognise and live with cultural diversity is a failure of imagination; a failure to look on human association in ways not ruled by these dubious images."[8] That failure stems in no small part from the legacy of John Locke and its entanglement with what Tully dubs "the empire of uniformity" of modern constitutionalism. The dubious images are those of a timeless and universal model of human society that he argues emerges from abstract rationalist theories of politics like those attributed to Locke and his influential concepts of consent, rights, and resistance.

It is indeed a failure of imagination to insist on a notion of reason as detached from social and material experience as the lone or dominant faculty for understanding and critically engaging our social and political conditions. Moreover, this failure of imagination is centrally tied to blindness to the plurality and contingency of social and political arrangements and relations. Locke's legacy has figured significantly in traditions of political thought that identify critique with a disavowal of the particular, contingent, and plural conditions of political life. The account of Locke's thought that has emerged over these past five chapters offers up a different legacy, however, that challenges the empire of uniformity and avows, even highlights, the plural, particular, and contingent conditions of critique. Instead, we find a model of reasoned critique that draws from the imaginative and affective force of rhetoric to reinvent our ways of relating to a past that does not always seem to give us the freedom we seek.

My interpretation offers the conditions for a new Lockean legacy of a theory and model of critique that responds to the call for imagination and diversity in modern democratic life. That is not to say that Locke is a champion of the kind of democratic and egalitarian modes of life that are needed today, any more than his feminine and foreign images are themselves useful representations for a late modern feminist or postcolonial politics. Rather, the model of Lockean critique that I have presented offers up resources for relating to social and political arrangements, even those that involve subjection, by building from those situated and particular conditions to open up the possibility of a future freedom. Such situated and inventive critique is appropriate to the demands of democratic life because it disavows neither the situated conditions of political judgment nor the possibility that those judgments might yield novel futures. Locke's situated political critique offers important resources for contesting those unfreeing elements in his political thought, especially those captured under the rubric of the sexual and racial contract.

Far from the privileging of uniformity and detachment, Locke's theory and practice of critique entails taking particular established figures and images and putting them before his readers' sight in new, multiple, and shifting forms. In some cases, these new forms signify dangerous pretentions to authority. In others, they reconceive political practices of consent and resistance. At its most powerful, Locke's inventive critique refigures the symbolic order of individual, social, and political life in ways that delegitimize some claims to authority and make possible new modes of authorization. Inventive critique, in this way, has the capacity to create new conditions for political claims of authority and resistance without a flight from the political to the Archimedean point. The work of rhetoric in Lockean critique makes possible new judgments about political authority and inaugurates new possibilities for a future political freedom.

What we have discovered in Locke's thought, where we may have least expected it, is the value of the ingenious and inventive capacities of rhetoric as a way of working from the material world—sensory, social, and political—without being bound to reproduce it. Rhetoric as imaginative language serves as the source of novelty that emerges from human activity when we draw from experience and use it to generate, enrich, and re-create the frameworks we use for judging. The use of figure, style, and invention that we have discovered in Locke's work is integral to bringing into sight the plurality constitutive of political life and thereby creating the conditions for critical judgment. It also offers resources for generating and transforming frameworks of judgment in the face of new situations, enabling a move from judgment as the subsumption of particulars or negotiation between existing opinions to judgment as critique. In this way, Lockean critique need not posit a radical break with history because experience in a broad sense, including but not limited to history, can be not only understood but also felt, to provide more than one possibility for the future. It is this plurality that Lockean critique does not resist but, rather, generates as its very condition of possibility.

Locke's *Essay* and the *Two Treatises* come unexpectedly to attest to some of the important ways that rhetoric as imaginative language contributes to critique. The combined work of Locke's claim to experience and his appropriation of rhetoric, each as important as the other, yields a mode of critique that forwards a practice of political imagination that does not leave behind the material conditions of politics. Imagination, no less than reason, can mark a flight from the embodied, social, and political world, as in utopian thought or thought experiments. Such flights of fancy can yield new ways of engaging political realities. That is not the political imagination that we have discovered in Locke's thought, however. Keeping the claim to experience at the center, as Locke does, generates an imaginative capacity that is built into the very nature of our social practices, our language, and our capacity to begin anew from within such conventions, once established. It resides particularly powerfully in the capacity to see our established practices in new ways, such that their repetition comes to produce something other than the past. In short, it is political imagination as critical activity that may include, but is never reducible to, particular social and political imaginaries.

Preface

1. Locke, *An Essay Concerning Human Understanding*, "The Epistle to the Reader," 10.

Chapter 1

1. I borrow this phrase from Dawson, who uses it to describe Locke's relationship to the trivium, the early modern curriculum that included rhetoric along with grammar and logic; see Dawson, *Locke, Language, and Early-Modern Philosophy*, 3.

2. Garsten, *Saving Persuasion*, 5.

3. Ibid., 198, 210.

4. Arendt, *On Revolution*, and "Understanding and Politics."

5. Rawls, *A Theory of Justice*, and *Political Liberalism*; Habermas, *Structural Transformation*; Benhabib, *The Claims of Culture*.

6. For imagination in Rawls's original position, compared with some of Locke's imaginative exercises, see Liebell, "Lockean Switching." On Habermas and rhetoric, see Arash Abizadeh, "Philosophy/Rhetoric Binaries."

7. On the irreducible fact of human plurality in politics, see Arendt, *The Human Condition*. On the various material conditions obscured by abstract individualism, see Macpherson, *The Political Theory of Possessive Individualism*; Pateman, *The Disorder of Women*; and Mills, *The Racial Contract*.

8. Grassi, *Rhetoric as Philosophy*, 20.

9. Ibid., 92, 9, 16, 45.

10. Norval, *Aversive Democracy*, 85–87. See Zerilli, *Feminism and the Abyss of Freedom*, 60–61, 90.

11. Grassi, *Rhetoric as Philosophy*, 33.

12. Ibid., 8.

13. Bakhtin speaks specifically of the novel, but what he draws from novelistic discourse are its rhetorical elements, which are not limited to the novel form. They are characteristic too of practical speech. While Locke's *Essay* is today taken as a canonical philosophical text, its genre of the essay form is meant to be a much more informal and occasional style, proceeding from its contingent situation. Moreover, Bakhtin argues that even texts written in a "'unitary language,' operate in the midst of heteroglossia" (Bakhtin, *The Dialogic Imagination*, 271).

14. This is not to argue, conversely, that it is impossible for theoretical argument and style to be at odds with one another or with a theorist's self-presentation as refusing rhetoric. Before concluding that Locke's arguments are undermined by his rhetoric, we much first consider if his arguments might not be instead transformed and understood differently in light of their mode of expression.

15. Sprat, *History of the Royal Society*, 62.

16. Ibid., 113.

17. Specifically, Sprat aligns the Royal Society with the interests of the Church of England and latitudinarians, or church moderates, as well as the recovery of Charles II's London after the fire. For a discussion of the political engagements of Sprat's *History of the Royal Society*, see Vickers, "The Royal Society," 6, 41–46, 51, 62.

18. Locke, *An Essay Concerning Human Understanding*. Hereafter, citations will include book, chapter, and paragraph numbers. On Locke's characterization of rhetoric as philosophy's gaudy dress, see Zerilli, "'Philosophy's Gaudy Dress.'" See also Carver's response, "Rhetoric and Fantasy Revisited," and Zerilli's "Response."

19. Locke, *Of the Conduct of the Understanding*, §32. Hereafter, this work will be abbreviated as *CU*.

20. Locke, *Some Thoughts Concerning Education*, §188. Hereafter, this work will be abbreviated as *STCE*. Locke's caution resisted both the more traditional Aristotelian/Ciceronian models and the less ornate Ramist style (Shapiro, *Probability and Certainty*, 253–54).

21. Kahn, *Wayward Contracts*, 135–51. For other theorists who have sought a new understanding of Hobbes's relationship to rhetoric, see Q. Skinner, *Reason and Rhetoric*, Martel, *Subverting Leviathan*, and D. Skinner, "Political Theory." Readers of Hobbes have long appreciated his masterful use of rhetoric. See, in particular, Johnston, *The Rhetoric of "Leviathan,"* and Herzog, *Happy Slaves*. On Hobbes's materialism, see Frost, *Lessons from a Materialist Thinker*.

22. Vickers overturns the thesis of R. F. Jones that there was a profound shift in mentality and an "organized revolt" against Puritan rhetoric around 1660; see Vickers, "The Royal Society," 10. Vickers, by contrast, offers "a model of a continuous series of disputes of a more or less partisan nature in which style or rhetoric or language is an element in a bigger quarrel" (ibid., 25). See also Jones, *The Seventeenth Century*, 143–64.

23. Vickers, "The Royal Society," 62.

24. Ibid., 11. Shapiro, *Probability and Certainty*, 234–35, 237.

25. Howell, "John Locke and the New Rhetoric," and Corbett, "John Locke's Contributions to Rhetoric."

26. Vickers, "The Royal Society," 8, 3.

27. Sprat, *History of the Royal Society*, 112.

28. Vickers, "The Royal Society," 8.

29. Clark, "'The Whole Internal World His Own,'" 243.

30. Locke's theory of language is performed, if also disavowed, in a manner more closely approximating Nietzsche's in "On Truth and Lies in a Extra-moral Sense" (de Man, "Epistemology of Metaphor," 22).

31. For an account of some of the figural language of Locke's major texts, see Richetti, *Philosophical Writing*, chap. 2. Richetti keenly observes rhetorical dimensions of empiricist philosophical writings. His readings, however, "do not claim to alter radically the established or received versions of the thought of Locke, Berkeley," deferring instead to "professional explanations of that thought" (47). Richetti wants to resist the de Manian frame that pits philosophy against rhetoric, but his deferral to "professional" philosophers fails to consider the productive power of rhetoric in generating philosophical arguments that do not necessarily cohere to received categories like empiricism or liberalism.

32. Lloyd, *The Man of Reason*.

33. See Macpherson, *The Political Theory of Possessive Individualism*; Pateman, *The Sexual Contract*; Mills, *The Racial Contract*; and Hirschmann, "Intersectionality."

34. Locke, *Two Treatises of Government*. Hereafter, citations will include book and section numbers.

35. On the rationalist and empiricist labeling of Locke's work, see Aarsleff, *From Locke to Saussure*. Further examples include the relative disregard for the *First Treatise* as a theoretical text that rises above the narrow concerns of a political debate with the work of Robert Filmer, a debate taken to be constrained by historical interests. The division of fact and fiction is a framework placed over the *Second Treatise* and, in particular, the state of nature and other examples of early and foreign societies. See, for example, Ashcraft, "Locke's State of Nature."

36. Laslett, introduction to Locke, *Two Treatises*, 84.

37. On the intertwined rationalist and empiricist tendencies of Locke's philosophy and latter-day efforts to categorize philosophers according to this distinction, see Aarsleff, *From Locke to Saussure*. On critical accounts of the treatment of Locke in the writing of philosophical histories, see Walker, *Locke, Literary Criticism, and Philosophy*, 14–18.

38. See, for example, Goldie, "The Revolution of 1689"; Tully, *An Approach to Political Philosophy*; and Pocock, *The Ancient Constitution*.

39. Marshall, *John Locke*; Wood, *The Politics of Locke's Philosophy*; Ashcraft, *Revolutionary Politics*; Dunn, *The Political Thought of John Locke*.

40. Locke scholars note the influence of Gassendi in various areas of Locke's thought, among them language, judgment, atomism, and hypothesis. See, for example, Ott, *Locke's Philosophy of Language*; Tully, "Governing Conduct"; Kroll, "The Question"; Lennon, *The Battle of the Gods and Giants*, 149–90.

41. Kroll, *The Material Word*. For a discussion of Epicurean materialism in the earlier phase of its recovery in the early modern period, see Greenblatt, *The Swerve*.

42. Grassi, *Rhetoric as Philosophy*, 8–10. See also Crusius's foreword to this work (xv).

43. This is not to make the strong claim that Locke adheres closely to a Ciceronian conception and practice of rhetoric. Rather, I gesture here to a continuity in the political philosophy of Locke and Cicero that is useful for conceptualizing the way that rhetoric can be understood to relate to experience. On Cicero as an influence for Locke, see Wood, *The Politics of Locke's Philosophy*, chaps. 1–2.

44. Tully, *Strange Multiplicity*, 58.

Chapter 2

1. Sellars, *Empiricism*, 33–34.

2. Rorty, *Philosophy and the Mirror of Nature*, 50–51.

3. Examples of this critique of empiricism are particularly evident in literary criticism that engages philosophical texts. In addition to Rorty, de Man, Caruth, and Law address Locke as a seminal influence in the empiricist tradition and its hostility to language. Like de Man, Caruth and Law show the indispensable role of language in empiricism, but they present this as an unwitting feature of Locke's text (Caruth, *Empirical Truths*, 1–43; Law, *The Rhetoric of Empiricism*, 1–92).

4. Aarsleff, *From Locke to Saussure*, 120–45.

5. Farr, "The Way of Hypotheses," 51. On the centrality of Locke's scientific concerns, see Yolton, *Locke and the Compass of Human Understanding*. On the Christian underpinnings of Locke's thought, see Dunn, *The Political Thought of John Locke*, and Tully, *A Discourse on Property*.

6. Taylor, *Sources of the Self*, 159–76, 234–47.

7. Yolton, *Locke and the Compass of Human Understanding*, 4–5. Yolton emphasizes the contextual importance of the Royal Society for Locke's *Essay*. Walmsley argues for the rhetorical influence of the "plain, historical method" on the *Essay* as a natural history of the human understanding (Walmsley, *Locke's "Essay"*).

8. Shapiro, *Probability and Certainty*, 5–6, 228.

9. On the trivium, see Dawson, *Locke, Language, and Early-Modern Philosophy*, part 1.

10. Shapiro, *Probability and Certainty*, 6–7.

11. Ibid., 230–31.

12. Conley, *Rhetoric in the European Tradition*, 125.

13. Ibid., 124–32. For an overview of English rhetorics from 1530 to 1600, see 133–43.

14. Shapiro, *Probability and Certainty*, 8.

15. Ibid., 229.

16. Conley, *Rhetoric in the European Tradition*, 152.

17. Shapiro, *Probability and Certainty*, 9 and also 14.

18. I borrow from Shapiro the phrase "early empirical scientists" to describe those seventeenth-century thinkers advancing the new experimental science. While this work may be seen as a precursor to subsequent empiricism, I do not mean to reassert this casting of Locke in the latter-day

philosophical school. *Early empirical science* refers to the more contextually specific emergence of new scientific practices in the seventeenth century (ibid., 15, 18).

19. Ibid., 37. Casson, *Liberating Judgment*, 101.

20. Shapiro, *Probability and Certainty*, 20–21, 20–23.

21. Ibid., 4.

22. Daston, *Classical Probability*; Serjeantson, "Testimony and Proof"; Shapiro, *Probability and Certainty*, 21.

23. Shapiro, *Probability and Certainty*, 37.

24. Shapin, *The Scientific Revolution*, 87.

25. Ibid., 108, 107–8; emphasis in original removed.

26. Casson, *Liberating Judgment*, 143, 147, 149.

27. In addition to Casson, *Liberating Judgment*, see Walker, *Locke, Literary Criticism, and Philosophy*, 110; Wolterstorff, *John Locke*; Tully, "Governing Conduct," 216.

28. Casson, *Liberating Judgment*, 146; Shapiro, *Probability and Certainty*, 42; Locke, *Essay* 4.3.18.

29. Casson, *Liberating Judgment*, 151, 157. Tully argues that "once Locke had mastered the concept of probability in 1676, he realized that a demonstrable ethics was no longer necessary: probability and opinion are sufficient for all our concernments." He cites Locke's journal entry on the wager in support; "Faith and reason" (1676), *Political Essays*, 248–50 (cited in Tully, "Governing Conduct," 216).

30. Walker, *Locke, Literary Criticism, and Philosophy*, 110. Locke, *Essay* 4.17.

31. McClure, *Judging Rights*, 45.

32. There are a number of interpretations of Locke's thought that bridge this purported gap, but they differ in their accounts of how they do so. Dunn and Tully emphasize the Christian foundations of Locke's thought, which Strauss fundamentally questions (Dunn, *The Political Thought of John Locke*; Tully, *A Discourse on Property*; Strauss, *Natural Right and History*). Grant (and Waldron, in his early work) emphasizes the foundational role of reason; see Grant, *John Locke's Liberalism*, and Waldron, "John Locke." Waldron goes on to ground that notion of reason in theological foundations in *God, Locke, and Equality*. Mehta provides an innovative version of the rational foundations of Locke's thought that emphasizes Locke's efforts to contain the unruliness of cognitive capacities, particularly of the imagination; see Mehta, *The Anxiety of Freedom*.

33. Shapiro argues that the early English empirical scientists took two general directions on the future of rhetoric in relation to their new scientific practices. Bacon and Hobbes, she argues, sought to eliminate rhetorical devices and poetic language in natural science and philosophy, allowing a reformed account of rhetoric to continue in civil life, moral discourse, ordinary conversation and poetry. By contrast, she sees Thomas Sprat and especially Locke pressing for the elimination of the philosophy-rhetoric dualism, yielding a single linguistic standard free of rhetoric and the deceptive force of eloquence. Shapiro focuses her examination of rhetoric in these thinkers primarily on their attacks. I will depart from Shapiro's view in arguing that the breakdown of the philosophy-rhetoric dualism in Locke cannot simply be captured by the subordination of rhetoric to philosophy. Rather, rhetoric comes to be appropriated in a fundamental role into Locke's understanding of rational thought and discourse (Shapiro, *Probability and Certainty*, 242–43).

34. As Farr argues, the ambiguity of the term *science* in Locke's *Essay* means that we cannot "readily determine the continuity or discontinuity which Locke thought existed between the various enterprises for the 'understanding,' say, medicine, natural religion, political knowledge, and the 'experimental Philosophy of physical Things'" (Farr, "The Way of Hypotheses," 52, citing Locke, *Essay* 4.3.26). Shapiro and Kroll demonstrate the very wide-ranging topics and areas of inquiry that came under the sway of probabilistic reasoning throughout their respective works.

35. Kroll, *The Material Word*, 52. Kroll's attention to the broader cultural shifts accompanying the rise of probability in the mid-seventeenth century is a corrective to Shapiro's account. Shapiro draws attention to the sources of probable judgment in the rhetorical tradition. She emphasizes how probability was reworked for a scientific outlook that stressed impartiality and the absence of bias (see Shapiro, *A Culture of Fact*, in particular). Kroll significantly expands on Shapiro's work by showing how rhetoric was integral to the enactment of new modes of judgment across the many fields of thought and writing where both writers see these changes playing out. This broader view

is particularly important for understanding a thinker like Locke who works in the scientific idiom of natural philosophy but is deeply concerned with language and politics.

36. Kroll, *The Material Word*, 114–15.

37. To identify this broad culture of Epicureanism, of which Gassendi was a primary articulator and influence, is not to say that all these ideas were shared in identical form by various thinkers. Hobbes, for example, does not share the interest in experience and observation as a source of knowledge that the early empirical scientists do. Moreover, his relationship with Gassendi is better characterized as one of mutual influence, between contemporaries and interlocutors. As we will see, Locke adopts many of these notions associated with a broader Epicurean materialist culture in his own distinctive constellation (Kroll, *The Material Word*, 15, 160–61; Sarasohn, "Motion and Morality," 364). For an account of Hobbes's anti-Cartesian materialism that does not emphasize the links to Gassendi, see Frost, *Lessons from a Materialist Thinker*.

38. Kroll, *The Material Word*, 127.

39. Shapiro, *Probability and Certainty*, 252–54.

40. Lucretius, *The Way Things Are*. Kroll describes how the relation is more than an analogy between letters as parts of words and atoms as components of the world: "Lucretius' almost obsessive punning on the parallel between atoms and letters elegantly collapses a series of arguments that relate language to the world" (Kroll, *The Material Word*, 11).

41. Kroll, *The Material Word*, 184, 193.

42. Ibid., 86. On the consciousness of artificiality in this period, see Foucault, *The Order of Things*, 4–16.

43. Kroll, *The Material Word*, 53.

44. Ibid., 53–55.

45. This reading of the epistle closely follows Kroll's in ibid., 52–55.

46. Shapiro, *Probability and Certainty*, 234. Bacon and Locke are otherwise distinguished by significant epistemological differences insofar as Bacon believed that the study of nature could reveal its essential truths. Locke took a more skeptical position that stopped short of direct knowledge of the inner workings of nature, which is discussed in the next chapter, on "substances."

47. Adorno, "The Essay as Form," 16. This quote is also cited in Panagia's discussion of the essay genre, inaugurated by Montaigne, in the tradition embracing paradox and an aesthetic of the grotesque, as theorized by Bakhtin in *Rabelais and His World*. From Montaigne, Panagia reminds us, Locke inherits a genre of mixture, natural and unnatural, that is always contingent, lacking in predetermined destination, and in its best versions, piecemeal. Adorno's depiction of the essay as a style of writing that emerges from within contingent, lived experience as a mode of critical engagement, as we will see, is well suited to Locke's work (Panagia, "The Force of Political Argument," 826–28; Adorno, "The Essay as Form," 18).

48. Walker shows how Locke invokes the language of acquaintance, which carries sexual connotations in Restoration libertine comedy, when he invites the reader into a pleasurable acquaintance with his or her own understanding: "But whatever be the Difficulties, that lie in the way of this Enquiry; . . . all the Acquaintance we can make with our own Understandings, will not only be very pleasant; but bring us great Advantage, in directing our Thoughts in the search of other things" (1.1.1). He continues this erotic and social imagery by figuring truth as "a Subject lying somewhat in the dark." With promises of pleasure and advantage, Locke invites the reader to follow him, proceeding from principles that appeal only to "Mens own unprejudiced *Experience*, and Observation, whether they be true, or no" (1.4.25) (Walker, *Locke, Literary Criticism, and Philosophy*, 68–71).

49. On the treatment of language in the trivium, the traditional curriculum of the schools, see Dawson, *Locke, Language, and Early-Modern Philosophy*. On various language philosophies emerging in the seventeenth century, see Lewis, *Language, Mind, and Nature*, and Formigari, *Language and Experience*.

50. De Man describes his process of reading at one point as one in which "rhetoric is a disruptive intertwining of trope and persuasion or—which is not quite the same thing—of cognitive and performative language" (*Allegories of Reading*, lx).

51. On the variety of appeals associated with innate ideas, see Yolton, *John Locke*, 26–53.

52. *CU*, §1.

53. See also 3.3.7 for an account of the child's move from particular to general ideas. Walker observes how female figures (of nurse and mother) recede with increasing levels of abstraction (Walker, *Locke, Literary Criticism, and Philosophy*, 62–63). Locke returns throughout the *Essay* to the figure of the child.

54. The trope of printing, involving the stamp of characters and impressions on the understanding, remains seemingly constant, but Locke reverses its meaning; see 1.2.5, 1.2.27, 1.3.22. On the figuring of experience as writing, see Law, *The Rhetoric of Empiricism*, ix, 50, 90.

55. On Locke's interest in travel literature and its place in his thought, see Carey, *Locke, Shaftesbury, and Hutcheson*, 71–92; Carey, "Travel, Geography, and the Problem of Belief"; and Arneil, *John Locke and America*, 21–44.

56. Montaigne, "Des cannibales." On the significance of the figure of the child in Montaigne's thought, see Regosin, *Montaigne's Unruly Brood*. Wootton emphasizes Locke's relationship to skepticism, and to Pierre Charron, a contemporary and follower of Montaigne, in particular, writing that Locke was "engaged in an intimate dialogue with skeptical themes, skeptical arguments, and, we must presume, skeptical authors," in his introduction to *John Locke* (29). Such Montaignean examples can also be found in the *Essays on the Law of Nature* and the *Two Tracts* (Wootton, introduction to *John Locke*, 27–31).

57. Yolton, *John Locke*, 4, 1, 10.

58. Carey, *Locke, Shaftesbury, and Hutcheson*, 71.

59. Experience is a limiting condition as much as an enabling one. As Locke continues, "but yet, I think, it will be granted easily, That if a Child were kept in a place, where he never saw any other but Black and White, till he were a Man, he would have no more *Ideas* of Scarlet or Green, than he that from his Childhood never tasted an Oyster, or a Pine-Apple, has of those particular Relishes" (2.1.6).

60. Jolley, *Locke*, 18. In labeling Locke an agnostic weak materialist, Jolley does not mean to attribute to him any religious agnosticism. Locke brackets "Physical Consideration of the Mind . . . or by what Motions of our Spirits, or Alterations of our Bodies, we come to have any Sensation by our Organs, or any *Ideas* in our Understandings; and whether those *Ideas* . . . depend on Matter or no" (1.1.12). To say that Locke marginalizes such questions does not mean that he never entertains possibilities of the inner workings of the human body and understanding, such as the way that simple sensory ideas are carried by sensory organs and nerves "to convey them from without to their Audience in the Brain, the mind's Presence-room" (2.3.1). Locke's atomistic assumptions tie him to a larger materialist culture even as he downplays the importance of metaphysical questions for his exploration of the conduct of the understanding. Locke's *Essay* proceeds on the assumption that we can conduct ourselves, our understandings, without certain knowledge of how the relations between external bodies, senses, and the understanding interact. It is this limited scope of the human understanding—even when we consider the understanding as an object of inquiry—that is a key component of Locke's Epicurean materialism.

61. On this Epicurean project of cautious and limited reconstruction, see Kroll, *The Material Word*, chap. 3.

62. Abrams, *The Mirror and the Lamp*, 63. As James notes, the idea of a mind transparent to itself is broadly, but often erroneously, applied more generally to early modern philosophers, including Locke as well as Descartes. See James, *Passion and Action*, 16–17.

63. James, *Passion and Action*, 166. See Locke, *Essay* 2.7.4. Locke expresses a view shared by many seventeenth-century philosophers: "our passions are designed to ensure that we attend to our well-being as embodied creatures" (James, *Passion and Action*, 186).

64. James, *Passion and Action*, 14.

65. In *Essay* 2.20 Locke explains a variety of passions, such as love, hatred, desire, hope, and fear, so that they all come down to two basic ideas of pain and pleasure, also called delight and uneasiness. In this way, he offers a reduced account of the passions in comparison with other authors, who see a more expansive range. Although James suggests that Locke offers an older account, his reduced version more closely resembles the stripped-down version she attributes to Hobbes (James, *Passion and Action*, 73). Envy and anger are both exceptions in that they are caused not only by pain and pleasure but also by ideas of other people and ourselves (2.20.14).

66. Locke continues this passage with a consideration of the material basis for memory, that is, whether it is a function of the body. Characteristically, he refuses to answer whether it is the temper of the brain, animal spirits, or some other bodily constitution that accounts for memory loss. Instead he cautions a probable judgment expressed in a series of especially material metaphors, suggesting that the fading pictures in our minds may be written in marble, freestone, or even sand. Locke refuses a single physical explanation for memory yet remains within the register of materialism and probable judgment.

67. For a fuller discussion of the similarity between madness and sanity in Locke, see Mehta, *The Anxiety of Freedom*, 112–14.

68. James calls this an error of projection in which "we commonly attribute internal movements, passions, to external things that seem to cause them" according to thinkers such as Descartes, Spinoza, and Malebranche. Lockean association reiterates some of these concerns (James, *Passion and Action*, 165–66).

69. Locke, journal entry from January 22, 1678, cited by Mehta, *The Anxiety of Freedom*, 108.

70. Mehta, *The Anxiety of Freedom*, 118.

71. The *Oxford English Dictionary* (*OED*) provides a catalog of the many ways that passion can be tied to volatile and overwhelming emotions as well as pain. In addition, it emerges from a notion of passivity, as when one is overcome and rendered passive by such a physical or emotional feeling. In this latter sense, it is contrasted with action and identified as "an effect produced by an external force" (*OED*, 2nd ed., s.v. "passion," 11a). Locke refuses to see association as caused by the power of an unruly passion, as Hobbes does, which leads Mehta to see association as unrelated to passions (Mehta, *The Anxiety of Freedom*, 112). Although Locke's view of how passions work on the understanding is different from that of Hobbes, we should not overlook the passionate nature of association.

72. This is not to suggest that there is no place for sensory or other forms of experience in these competing philosophical accounts, particularly Aristotelianism. Rather, Locke's critique of innatism and the unruliness of the subjects' perceptual and cognitive capacities trouble the tie between perceptual experience and universal forms.

Chapter 3

1. The body is no less a condition of consciousness than the mind as Locke gives some, but not much, priority to ideas of sensation (2.1.10). Sensation occurs before reflection in a child, for example. Sensation alone, however, is insufficient for the reasonable understanding that Locke goes on to develop.

2. Consciousness emerges from memory to make possible a subject recognizable to itself and to law. In short, Locke does not believe that the disruptions to consciousness prevent a sense of self from emerging over time, nor do they erode moral and legal responsibility (2.27.10).

3. Locke initially introduces the understanding and the will as distinct human capacities (2.21.5), but the will ultimately depends on the understanding. Rather than treating the subject as composed of multiple faculties as if they were plural agents, Locke urges us to see faculties as tied to a capacity of a single subject to act or not (2.21.20).

4. For two accounts that emphasize the centrality of this problematic of judgment across Locke's writings, see McClure, *Judging Rights*, and Casson, *Liberating Judgment*.

5. Kroll, "The Question," 401. Tully, "Governing Conduct," 207.

6. James, *Passion and Action*. Part 3 examines these various strategies and chap. 8 addresses scientia in particular.

7. Ibid., 215–21.

8. James presents Hobbes as the exemplary figure. While there is evidence for this depiction, Kahn shows how Hobbes's political contract, based in materialist reasoning, is conditioned upon a particular rhetorical understanding, that is, a linguistic contract (Kahn, *Wayward Contracts*, 137).

9. James, *Passion and Action*, 225–32.

10. *CU*, §1. See Shuger, *Sacred Rhetoric*.

11. On Locke's commitment to public judgment in the *Essay* in contrast to Montaigne, see Casson, *Liberating Judgment*, 9, 54, 92–93. I depart here from Casson's depiction of Montaigne as undermining judgment. On the importance of judgment in Montaigne's work, see Hartle, *Michel de Montaigne*.

12. Tully, "Governing Conduct," 231–32, 233, citing Locke, *CU*, §§11–12.

13. Ibid., 222.

14. Locke devotes §§2–30 to habits of the body. In §31 he turns to the mind, but the passages continuing until §133 include a broad range of topics, including passions, judgment, and temperament, as well as the effects of physical conditions, such as corporal punishment, on the development of character and reason. The interplay of body and mind is dramatically captured in Locke's phrase the "physiognomy of the mind" (§101).

15. Locke calls the fables "the only book almost that I know fit for children" (*STCE*, §189).

16. Egalitarian among the select class of the sons, and potentially daughters for the most part, of gentlemen for whom Locke intends his education. There is no indication that this is meant for society as a whole. On the exclusions of Locke's education, see Hirschmann, "Intersectionality."

17. For a discussion of Locke's recommendation of fables in his letters to Edward Clark, which evolved into *STCE*, see McClure, "Cato's Retreat," 329–30.

18. Although it is beyond the scope of this chapter, it is worth noting that Chillingworth, the seventeenth-century English humanist, applies rhetorical standards of probability to matters of religion. For a discussion of his contributions to toleration and the connection to Locke's work on toleration, see Remer, *Humanism*, 137–68, 231–41.

19. Casson, *Liberating Judgment*, 94–95, 172–73, 181. See also Tully, "Governing Conduct," 216.

20. The need to make claims and understand such matters beyond the scope of sensory perception is captured, at least in part, by the question of the role of hypothesis in Locke's thought. Where Yolton emphasizes only a Baconian focus on observation and experience as the hallmark of the *Essay*, Farr, Kroll, and Lauden argue persuasively for the ineliminable role of hypothesis in Locke's thought. Recognizing the value of hypothesis links Locke to both Boyle and Gassendi (Yolton, *Locke and the Compass of Human Understanding*; Farr, "The Way of Hypotheses"; Kroll, "The Question," 401; Laudan, "The Nature and Sources").

21. On Locke's support for analogy in scientific thinking and especially experiment, see *CU*, §40.

22. Vogt, *John Locke*, 21. Much of Vogt's reading depends on the passages of the *Essay* cited here. He draws additional evidence from his reading of Locke's "An Examination of Malebranche's Opinion," sec. 41.

23. Vogt, *John Locke*, 20.

24. Brown, "The 'Figure' of God."

25. Shuger, *Sacred Rhetoric*, 11–12.

26. For an account of Locke on this distinction, see Vogt, *John Locke*, 26. On the seventeenth-century phenomenon, particularly within the New Science, see Vickers, "The Royal Society," 21–24.

27. Locke plays the Platonic definition against the Aristotelian one in this section of the *Essay*, dramatizing the plurality of notions inherited from the classical tradition. For a more extended discussion of these plural definitions, see Shanks, "Toleration and Democratic Membership."

28. Locke sees nature as playing a role in resemblances, but similarities can be as confusing as anomalies insofar as they both can confound existing categories of species (3.3.14). With substances, humans must actively affirm the qualities that define an object or being rather than passively receiving the complex idea; Dawson, *Locke, Language, and Early-Modern Philosophy*, 203–4.

29. Tuveson, "Locke and the Dissolution of the Ego," 165–66.

30. Dawson, *Locke, Language, and Early-Modern Philosophy*, 250.

31. De Man, "Epistemology of Metaphor," 22–23.

32. I borrow the phrase "material word" from Kroll, *The Material Word*.

33. Dawson, *Locke, Language, and Early-Modern Philosophy*, 251.

34. Ibid.

35. Dawson points out that Locke stands in contrast to Descartes and Spinoza in that he does *not* banish language from thought (Dawson, *Locke, Language, and Early-Modern Philosophy*, 256).

While he seeks to keep thought prior to language, "in practice the two are disturbingly tangled" (255).

36. As Walker writes, "This passage is an empiricist elaboration of Cicero's claim, in the third book of *On the Orator*, that 'the metaphorical employment of words was begun because of poverty' and that 'when something that can scarcely be conveyed by the proper term is expressed metaphorically, the meaning we desire to convey is made clear by the resemblance of the thing that we have expressed by the word that does not belong.' For Locke here asserts that many words which were originally used to stand for ideas derived from the sensation of outward objects were and still are used to stand for ideas which are derived from the mind's perception of its own operations (ideas of reflection)" (Walker, *Locke, Literary Criticism, and Philosophy*, 117).

37. Ibid., 118. *CU*, §32.

38. Dawson, *Locke, Language, and Early-Modern Philosophy*, 188.

39. Walker, *Locke, Literary Criticism, and Philosophy*, 120, 121.

40. Dawson, *Locke, Language, and Early-Modern Philosophy*, 260.

41. Ibid., 236.

42. Ibid., 250, citing *CU*, §9.

43. This is notable because Locke wrote against a backdrop of universal language schemes that aspired to reinvent ordinary speech in precisely the way that Locke ridicules and rejects.

44. Tully, "Governing Conduct," 225–29.

45. Casson, *Liberating Judgment*, 160–64.

46. I have in mind here Mehta, *The Anxiety of Freedom*; Tully, "Governing Conduct"; Casson, *Liberating Judgment*; and Dawson, *Locke, Language, and Early-Modern Philosophy*.

47. Dawson, in "Locke on Language," cites three fundamental ways that Locke's theory of language undermines his account of civil society: first, "the God-given sociability of man," second, the social contract (420), and third, a broader sense of shared culture (422).

48. Dawson, *Locke, Language, and Early-Modern Philosophy*, 218.

49. Ibid., 214.

Chapter 4

1. I take up the *First Treatise* here as an obviously related but distinct text in its own right. The publication history of the *Two Treatises* suggests that the two texts can be read as one or two works. Laslett, introduction to Locke, *Two Treatises*, 4–14. Wootton emphasizes the different political contexts and aims of these two texts; see his introduction to *John Locke*, 52.

2. Filmer, *Patriarcha*.

3. Tarlton, "A Rope of Sand," 46.

4. On the poor reception of the *First Treatise*, see ibid., 43–47. Mehta depicts the *First Treatise* as "among the most neglected, indeed maligned, major portion of an otherwise celebrated and much discussed body of work in political theory" (Mehta, *The Anxiety of Freedom*, 37–39). See also Waldron, *God, Locke, and Equality*, 16. Mehta and Waldron see intellectual significance in the *First Treatise* despite what they take as Locke's preoccupations with minutiae. Zuckert appreciates its value and blames Filmer for the tiresome quality of the refutations, placing him closer to Locke's own claims (Zuckert, "An Introduction," 121).

5. Schochet, *Patriarchalism*, 7.

6. Butler, "Early Liberal Roots of Feminism," 149.

7. Waldron, *God, Locke, and Equality*, 6.

8. Pateman, *The Sexual Contract*, 48–49.

9. Pateman, *The Disorder of Women*, 46.

10. Ibid., 53. Lloyd, *The Man of Reason*.

11. The language of covert/overt to describe modes of gendering in Locke's texts comes from Carver, "Gender and Narrative," 188–89.

12. Arneil, "Women as Wives, Servants, and Slaves."

13. Hirschmann, "Intersectionality."

14. Carver, "Gender and Narrative," 199–206.

15. My interest in reading Locke's feminine figures, in particular, is inspired by feminist theorists who emphasize the signifying or symbolic power of "woman" in a text rather than solely inquiring into what entity ("women,") the text refers to. See, for example, Wingrove, *Rousseau's Republican Romance*, 3–23, and Zerilli, *Signifying Woman*, 1–15.

16. "Fatherhood" appears seven times in *Patriarcha*, but only two cast the fatherhood as a possessive subject (1.8, 2.1). The others refer to "the right of fatherhood," after the extinction of the fatherhood (1.3, 8, 9, 2.1).

17. Laslett, introduction to Locke, *Two Treatises*, 57–59. *Patriarcha* may have been written in the 1620s (Tuck, "A New Date"). According to Laslett, Locke did not see *Patriarcha* until 1680, after beginning the *Second Treatise*. Ashcraft, Marshall, and Wootton disagree, contending that the *Second Treatise* was begun after the major part of the *First Treatise* was completed, though they disagree on how much later. They agree that work on the *First Treatise* began after January 1680 but not about how long composition lasted. Wootton believes it was completed by 1681 with some later additions. Marshall argues for mid- or late 1681, and Milton for earlier in mid-1680, but Scott argues that it was not written before late 1681 (Ashcraft, *Revolutionary Politics*; Marshall, *John Locke*; Wootton, introduction to *John Locke*, 63; Milton, "Dating Locke's Second Treatise"; Scott, "The Law of War," 572).

18. Living on beyond the author is a trait of another key seventeenth-century royalist text, Charles I's *Eikon Basilike*, published upon Charles's execution (Charles I, *Eikon Basilike*, 13).

19. Tarlton, "A Rope of Sand," 54.

20. Zwicker, *Lines of Authority*, 158.

21. *OED*, 2nd ed.

22. Locke acknowledges alternatives to Filmer, such as Sibthorpe or Manwaring (1.5). Schochet accords Filmer sufficient significance to warrant Locke's attention: "The Filmerian position very nearly became the official state ideology" (Schochet, *Patriarchalism*, 193). Daly, however, emphasizes Filmer's distance from conventional royalism (Daly, *Sir Robert Filmer*, 162).

23. Locke's reconstruction of Filmer's rhetoric aligns *Patriarcha* with court-style speech and "the corruption and exaggeration of a court that bows steadily in the direction of French manners and morals" (Zwicker, *Lines of Authority*, 159).

24. Waldron argues the opposite, pitting Locke's generalist egalitarianism against Filmer's particularist inegalitarianism and overlooking Locke's critique of patriarchalism's timeless universalism; see Waldron, *God, Locke, and Equality*, 22.

25. Zwicker, *Lines of Authority*, 160.

26. Filmer's position here is reported by Locke, not drawn directly from *Patriarcha*.

27. Locke is ambivalent on Eve and her significance for women. He argues that Eve's curse has implications for "the female Sex only, and import no more but that Subjection they should ordinarily be in to their Husbands." Rejecting the absolute authority of Adam, he emphasizes the contingent and contractual nature of marriage yet concludes that "there is . . . Foundation in Nature for" the subordination of wives (1.47). See also Carver, "Gender and Narrative," 193–98.

28. On the supplement, see Derrida, *Of Grammatology*, 141–60.

29. The affinity I emphasize here is not the use of Eve to show the error of patriarchalism (which Pateman would acknowledge) but the recollection of Eve as missing mother to destabilize the opposition's clam to universality.

30. Frye, *Anatomy of Criticism*, 224.

31. Parody is "the critical refunctioning of preformed literary material with comic effect" (Phiddian, *Swift's Parody*, 19, see also Rose, *Parody*, 35). Satire and parody both may render their target the object of laughter, but satire does not necessarily entail the imitation, distortion, or citation of external material; see Rose, *Parody*, 81–82.

32. Locke is well recognized as an object of satire and parody, but not for engaging in such styles himself (Zwicker, *Lines of Authority*, 161; Phiddian, *Swift's Parody*, 122–27).

33. Laslett attributes this point to Locke's medical training; see Locke, *Two Treatises*, 178n. A broader debate over theories of reproduction also plays out in the *First Treatise* (Greenfield,

"Aborting the 'Mother Plot,'" 269). This Aristotelian tradition features many cases of maternal activity in reproduction, often tied to a maternal imagination that yields monsters (Huet, *Monstrous Imagination*, 37–45).

34. For a detailed discussion of how Locke negotiates the political stakes of these views of reproduction in the case of monstrous births that arise in his *Essay*, see Shanks, "Toleration and Democratic Membership."

35. This passage echoes an earlier medical claim contrasting Eve's condition with subsequent mothers: "[T]here is here [in Eve's curse] no more Law to oblige a Woman to such a Subjection, if the Circumstances either of her condition or Contract with her Husband should exempt her from it, then there is, that she should bring forth her Children in Sorrow and Pain, if there could be found a Remedy for it" (1.47).

36. On the double character of monstrosity, see Girard, *Violence and the Sacred*, 160-65. Locke continues the contrast with his medical authority by depicting Filmer as the physician who covers the bitter taste of his tonic with deceptive palliatives, that is, with "mere" rhetoric (1.7).

37. Locke refers to a French translation of Garcilaso de la Vega's *Commentarios Reales: Le commentaire royal, ou l'Histoire des Yncas, roys du Peru*, trans. Jean Baudoin (Paris, 1633). The English translation is Locke's own (Carey, *Locke, Shaftesbury, and Hutcheson*, 72n6, 92–93; Locke, *Two Treatises*, 277n). On the evidence for the practices described by Garcilaso and his rhetorical appropriation of earlier texts, see Ross, "'A Very Knowing American.'"

38. Locke's critiques of innate ideas in the *Essay* and patriarchalism both draw on travel literature, specifically Garcilaso, to show the unbounded plurality of human ideas and practices to challenge universalist claims (1.3.9–12).

39. Frye, *Anatomy of Criticism*, 224. As iconic satirist John Dryden writes, "The true end of satire is the amendment of vices by correction" (Dryden, "Absalom and Achitophel," lines 72–73).

40. This reading resonates with Wright's interpretation of Locke's midwifery notes as presenting a notion of the family as "traditionally hierarchical, oriented to propagating the human species and the passing down of property" (Wright, "Recovering Locke's Midwifery Notes," 216).

41. For another list of heirs and ensuing questions of legitimacy, see 1.123: "Who has the *Paternal Power*, whilst the Widow-Queen is with Child by the deceased King, and no body knows whether it will be a Son or a Daughter? Which shall be Heir of two Male-Twins, who by the Dissection of the Mother, were laid open to the World?" Again Locke invokes medical knowledge of pregnancy, specifically cesarean section, to challenge the Fatherhood. Thanks to an anonymous reviewer for *Political Theory* for drawing this to my attention.

42. For Locke and Shaftesbury, the illegitimate son of Charles II, the duke of Monmouth, was a more suitable heir to the throne than was Charles's brother, James (Laslett, introduction to Locke, *Two Treatises*, 31–33, 123; Ashcraft, *Revolutionary Politics*, 286–87).

43. Ashcraft, *Revolutionary Politics*, 349. The poem was published at the height of the Exclusion Crisis. The poem is an allegory for the political controversy and takes particular aim at Shaftesbury, figured as Achitophel (Zwicker, *Lines of Authority*, 164). Marshall writes that Locke surely read the poem of 1681, citing Wootton that the poem "reflects an intellectual situation to which Locke needed to respond at a time of alleged composition [of the *Second Treatise*] in 'summer and autumn' 1681" (Marshall, *John Locke*, 146, 236, also 199–200). My argument does not depend on Locke's having read the poem, but it is worth noting that the poem's publication coincides with Marshall's and Scott's time frames for the composition of the *First Treatise*.

44. Dryden, "Absalom," line 1013. I rely here on the interpretations of Zwicker, *Lines of Authority*, 142, and Greenfield, "Aborting the 'Mother Plot,'" 285–87.

45. Ashcraft, *Revolutionary Politics*, 7.

Chapter 5

1. Laslett, introduction to Locke, *Two Treatises*, 84.

2. The idea that there are "two Lockes" has been challenged by a number of interpreters who reject this riven characterization of Locke's (il)logic, most often emphasizing reason, religion, or a

combination of the two as a deeper foundation on which to build a coherent Lockean philosophy. Such strategies, however, generally do not depart from the assumption that Locke's political thought requires a foundation outside human experience, particularly outside politics, to serve as the grounds for critique. Tully and Dunn find this common ground in Locke's religious assumptions, in particular his grounding in natural law; see Tully, *A Discourse on Property*, and Dunn, *The Political Thought of John Locke*. Grant, in *John Locke's Liberalism*, argues that the rationality of the *Essay* undergirds Locke's political thought. Waldron, in *God, Locke, and Equality* (in contrast to his earlier essay on the political anthropology and social contract discussed below), and Marshall articulate an interdependent relation between these rationalist and religious foundations. See Waldron, *God, Locke, and Equality*, and Marshall, *John Locke*.

3. Dawson, "Locke on Language," 398.

4. As evidence about consent and the state of nature, he cites Joseph Acosta's account of Brazil and Peru along with the foundings of Rome and Venice, among other examples (2.102–3). As evidence for the rise of monarchies from paternal authority, he looks to the Amerindians (2.105, 108) as well as the biblical figure of Jephtha (2.109). On the range of Locke's anthropological examples and sources from which he draws, see Batz, "The Historical Anthropology."

5. Batz and Grant give substantial attention to the examples, while Waldron is primarily concerned with the narrative (Batz, "The Historical Anthropology"; Grant, "Locke's Political Anthropology"; Waldron, "John Locke").

6. Grant, "Locke's Political Anthropology," 49.

7. Brennan and Pateman, "'Mere Auxiliaries'"; Pateman, *The Disorder of Women*; Carver, "Gender and Narrative." Seliger reconciles the political anthropology with Lockean consent to argue for a blurred distinction between liberalism and authoritarian rule or conservatism; see *The Liberal Politics of John Locke*, 210.

8. Grant, "Locke's Political Anthropology"; Waldron, "John Locke."

9. Waldron, "John Locke," 57.

10. Ibid.

11. Ibid., 63. Grant's argument that "Locke's individualism is a political individualism at the level of normative theory" in contrast to his recognition of the historical evidence of human interdependence and hierarchy enacts a similar division; see Grant, "Locke's Political Anthropology," 50, 51–52.

12. Kant, *Critique of Judgment*, 18–19.

13. For a reading that focuses on the examples, but not the longer narrative, see Carey, *Locke, Shaftesbury, and Hutcheson*, 92–97.

14. McClure, "Cato's Retreat," 328, citing Sidney, *Defense of Poetry*, 29.

15. Ibid.

16. Ibid., 331.

17. Ibid., 334.

18. Seth, *Europe's Indians*, 56. Locke cites Acosta's *The naturall and morall historie of the Indies* (1604), translated by Edward Grimestone (2.102).

19. Seth, *Europe's Indians*, 44–45. I am grateful to Kirstie McClure for first suggesting Locke's Ovidian formulation in chapter 5 of the *Second Treatise*.

20. Seth denies that Locke's state of nature has any connection to Ovid or Herodotus. I agree that Locke's appeals to a golden age may not share much more substantive agreement than this rhetorical convention, but there is nonetheless a coincidence of older and newer rhetorical styles in the *Second Treatise*. Tending to this stylistic heterogeneity opens up new ways of understanding Lockean critique that challenge the masterful rationality Seth attributes to Locke (Seth, *Europe's Indians*, 94–95).

21. McClure treats the examples and the narrative of the political anthropology all as narratives, more or less extended. I concur in the plurality of narratives she finds in the political anthropology, but in this reading, I stop short of considering each example as a narrative in itself because it loses sight of the replaying of similar narratives (McClure, "Cato's Retreat," 327–28). For accounts that address the narrative quality of the *Second Treatise*, within a single narrative framework, see Mehta, *The Anxiety of Freedom*; Dienstag, *Dancing in Chains*, part 1; and Zerilli, "'Philosophy's Gaudy Dress.'"

22. In Casson's words, the natural law "seems to be both present and absent in his account" (Casson, *Liberating Judgment*, 228, 228–29).

23. McClure, *Judging Rights*, 141. For a compatible account of how these passages contribute to a mode of judgment based on visible and tangible experience, see Casson, *Liberating Judgment*, 223–33.

24. According to the *OED*, *fancy* in the early modern period was used synonymously with *imagination* both as the "faculty of forming mental representations of things not present to the senses" and in the creative sense of producing images of things that do not exist. *Fancy* could also be used to indicate an invention or original contrivance, a usage that Locke also adopts (2.36, 48).

25. Casson, *Liberating Judgment*, 223.

26. Ibid., 225–26.

27. Laslett, introduction to Locke, *Two Treatises*, 68.

28. On the language of consent in the seventeenth century and its various sources, see Kahn, *Wayward Contracts*, 55.

29. Tully, "Rediscovering America," in *An Approach to Political Philosophy*; Arneil, *John Locke and America*; Pateman, *The Sexual Contract*; Pateman and Mills, *Contract and Domination*.

30. As Pocock argues, reference to the ancient constitution "formed one of the century's chief modes of political argument." Locke is the exception for not devoting parts of his writing to it; see Pocock, *The Ancient Constitution*, 46. See also Q. Skinner, *The Foundations of Modern Political Thought*, xiv.

31. The notion that the identification of the ancient constitution with custom goes so far back in time that it precedes memory served as an argument for limiting the power of the sovereign to it. Whichever institution came first—the king or the ancient constitution—was presumed to be the preeminent authority. By the seventeenth century, this argument was adapted as a defense of parliamentary sovereignty (Pocock, *The Ancient Constitution*, 49).

32. Pocock suggests a strain within ancient constitution arguments that does not argue for the existing constitution as immemorial custom (and thus protected from interference by the sovereign) but instead emphasizes the originary freedom and sovereignty of the people to arrange their constitution to suit their convenience (ibid., 21). By sharply distinguishing Locke from the ancient constitution writers, Pocock overlooks an affinity between this strain of argument and the elements of the *Second Treatise* treated here as the political anthropology.

33. Casson, *Liberating Judgment*, 19. See also Grant, "Locke's Political Anthropology," 52.

34. Dienstag, *Dancing in Chains*, 25.

35. Ibid., 26.

Conclusion

1. Brennan and Pateman, "'Mere Auxiliaries'"; Pateman, *The Sexual Contract*; Mills, *The Racial Contract*; Pateman and Mills, *Contract and Domination*.

2. Mills, *Racial Contract*. See also Shanks, "Consent."

3. Carey, *Locke, Shaftesbury, and Hutcheson*, 71. For an account of an even greater array of uses of examples of Americans across Locke's writings, serving diverse purposes, see Farr, "Locke, 'Some Americans,' and the Discourse on 'Carolina.'"

4. Seth, *Europe's Indians*, 99–100. For two accounts of how Locke represents indigenous peoples as part of a prepolitical past, see Rogin, "Liberal Society"; Benhabib, *The Claims of Culture*, 22–23, 42–47.

5. Seth, *Europe's Indians*, 99.

6. Ibid., 95; emphasis in original.

7. Hsueh, "Cultivating and Challenging the Common"; Arneil, *John Locke and America*, 23, 202; Tully, *An Approach to Political Philosophy*, chap. 5.

8. Tully, *Strange Multiplicity*, 201.

BIBLIOGRAPHY

Aarsleff, Hans. *From Locke to Saussure: Essays on the Study of Language and Intellectual History.* Minneapolis: University of Minnesota Press, 1982.

Abizadeh, Arash. "On the Philosophy/Rhetoric Binaries, Or Is Habermasian Discourse Motivationally Impotent?" *Philosophy and Social Criticism* 33, no. 4 (2007): 445-472.

Abrams, Meyer H. *The Mirror and the Lamp: Romantic Theory and the Critical Tradition.* New York: Oxford University Press, 1971.

Adorno, Theodor. "The Essay as Form." In *Notes to Literature*, vol. 1, 3–23. New York: Columbia University Press, 1991.

Arendt, Hannah. *The Human Condition.* Chicago: University of Chicago Press, 1970.

———. *On Revolution.* New York: Penguin, 1963.

———. "Understanding and Politics (The Difficulties of Understanding)." In *Essays in Understanding, 1930–1954*, 307–27. New York: Harcourt, Brace, 1994.

Armitage, David. "John Locke, Carolina, and the *Two Treatises of Government.*" *Political Theory* 32, no. 5 (2004): 602–27.

Arneil, Barbara. *John Locke and America: The Defense of English Colonialism.* Oxford: Clarendon, 1996.

———. "Women as Wives, Servants, and Slaves: Rethinking the Public/Private Divide." *Canadian Journal of Political Science* 44, no. 1 (2001): 29–54.

Ashcraft, Richard. "Locke's State of Nature: Historical Fact or Moral Fiction?" *American Political Science Review* 62, no. 3 (1968): 898–915.

———. *Locke's "Two Treatises of Government."* London: Allen & Unwin, 1987.

———. *Revolutionary Politics and Locke's "Two Treatises of Government."* Princeton: Princeton University Press, 1986.

Bakhtin, Mikhail. *The Dialogic Imagination.* Translated by Caryl Emerson and Michael Holquist. Austin: University of Texas Press, 1982.

———. *Rabelais and His World.* Translated by Hélène Iswolsky. Bloomington: Indiana University Press, 1984.

Balibar, Etienne. *Identity and Difference: John Locke and the Invention of Consciousness.* Translated by Warren Montag. London: Verso, 2013.

Batz, W. G. "The Historical Anthropology of John Locke." *Journal of the History of Ideas* 35, no. 4 (1974): 663–70.

Benhabib, Seyla. *The Claims of Culture: Equality and Diversity in the Global Era.* Princeton: Princeton University Press, 2002.

Bennington, Geoffrey. "The Perfect Cheat: Locke and Empiricism's Rhetoric." In *The Figural and the Literal: Problems of Language in the History of Science and Philosophy, 1630–1800*, edited by Andrew E. Benjamin, Geoffrey N. Cantor, and John R. R. Christie. Manchester: Manchester University Press, 1987.

Brennan, Teresa, and Carole Pateman. "'Mere Auxiliaries to the Commonwealth': Women and the Origins of Liberalism." *Political Studies* 27, no. 2 (1979): 183–200.

Brown, Vivienne. "The 'Figure' of God and the Limits to Liberalism: A Rereading of Locke's *Essay* and *Two Treatises.*" *Journal of the History of Ideas* 60, no. 1 (1999): 83–100.

Butler, Melissa. "Early Liberal Roots of Feminism: John Locke and the Attack on Patriarchy." *American Political Science Review* 72, no. 1 (1978): 135–50.

Carey, Daniel. *Locke, Shaftesbury, and Hutcheson: Contesting Diversity in the Enlightenment and Beyond*. Cambridge: Cambridge University Press, 2006.

———. "Travel, Geography, and the Problem of Belief." In *History and Nation*, edited by Julia Rudolph, 97–136. Lewisburg: Bucknell University Press.

Caruth, Cathy. *Empirical Truths and Critical Fictions: Locke, Wordsworth, Kant, Freud*. Baltimore: Johns Hopkins University Press, 1991.

Carver, Terrell. "Gender and Narrative in Locke's *Two Treatises of Government*." In *Feminist Interpretations of John Locke*, edited by Nancy Hirschmann and Kirstie McClure, 187–212. University Park: Pennsylvania State University Press, 2007.

———. "Rhetoric and Fantasy Revisited: A Response to Zerilli's 'Philosophy's Gaudy Dress.'" *European Journal of Political Theory* 5, no. 4 (2006): 469–77.

Casson, Douglas. *Liberating Judgment: Fanatics, Skeptics, and John Locke's Politics of Probability*. Princeton: Princeton University Press, 2011.

Charles I. *Eikon Basilike*. Edited by Jim Daems and Holly Faith Nelson. Peterborough, Ontario, Canada: Broadview, 2006.

Clark, S. H. "'The Whole Internal World His Own': Locke and Metaphor Reconsidered." *Journal of the History of Ideas* 59, no. 2 (1998): 241–65.

Colie, Rosalie. "The Social Language of John Locke: A Study in the History of Ideas." *Journal of British Studies* 4, no. 2 (1965): 29–51.

Conley, Thomas. *Rhetoric in the European Tradition*. Chicago: University of Chicago Press, 1994.

Corbett, Edward P. J. "John Locke's Contributions to Rhetoric." *College Composition and Communication* 32, no. 4 (1981): 423–33.

Daly, James. *Sir Robert Filmer and English Political Thought*. Toronto: University of Toronto Press, 1979.

Daston, Lorraine. *Classical Probability in the Enlightenment*. Princeton: Princeton University Press, 1988.

———. "Fear and Loathing of the Imagination in Science." *Daedalus* 127, no. 1 (1998): 73–95.

Dawson, Hannah. *Locke, Language, and Early-Modern Philosophy*. Cambridge: Cambridge University Press, 2007.

———. "Locke on Language in (Civil) Society." *History of Political Thought* 26, no. 3 (2005): 397–425.

De Man, Paul. *Allegories of Reading: Figural Language in Rousseau, Nietzsche, Rilke, and Proust*. New Haven: Yale University Press, 1979.

———. "Epistemology of Metaphor." *Critical Inquiry* 5, no. 1 (1978): 13–30.

Derrida, Jacques. *Of Grammatology*. Baltimore: Johns Hopkins University Press, 1997.

Dienstag, Joshua Foa. *Dancing in Chains: Narrative and Memory in Political Theory*. Stanford: Stanford University Press, 1997.

Dilts, Andrew. "To Kill a Thief: Punishment, Proportionality, and Criminal Subjectivity in Locke's *Second Treatise*." *Political Theory* 40, no. 1 (2012): 58–83.

Drury, Shadia. "Locke and Nozick on Property." *Political Studies* 30, no. 1 (1982): 28–41.

Dryden, John. "Absalom and Achitophel." In *Selected Poems*, edited by Steven N. Zwicker and David Bywaters, 111–41. New York: Penguin, 2001.

Dunn, John. "Consent in the Political Theory of John Locke." *Historical Journal* 10 (1967): 153–82.

———. *The Political Thought of John Locke: An Historical Account of the Argument of the "Two Treatises of Government."* Cambridge: Cambridge University Press, 1969.

———. "What Is Living and What Is Dead in John Locke?" In *Interpreting Political Responsibility: Essays, 1981–1989*, 9–25. Cambridge: Polity Press, 1990.

Farr, James. "Locke, Natural Law, and New World Slavery." *Political Theory* 36, no. 4 (2008): 495–522.

———. "Locke, 'Some Americans,' and the Discourse on 'Carolina.'" *Locke Studies* 9 (2009): 19–96.

———. "The Way of Hypotheses: Locke on Method." *Journal of the History of Ideas* 48, no. 1 (1987): 51–72.

Filmer, Robert. *Patriarcha and Other Writings*. Cambridge: Cambridge University Press, 1991.

Formigari, Lia. *Language and Experience in Seventeenth-Century British Philosophy.* Philadelphia: John Benjamins, 1988.

Foucault, Michel. *The Order of Things.* New York: Random House, 1970.

Frost, Samantha. *Lessons from a Materialist Thinker: Hobbesian Reflections on Ethics and Politics.* Stanford: Stanford University Press, 2008.

Frye, Northrop. *Anatomy of Criticism: Four Essays.* New York: Atheneum, 1966.

Garsten, Bryan. *Saving Persuasion: A Defense of Rhetoric and Judgment.* Cambridge: Harvard University Press, 2006.

Goldie, Mark. Introduction to *Two Treatises of Government,* by John Locke, xv–xliii. Edited by Mark Goldie. London: J. M. Dent, 1993.

———. "The Revolution of 1689 and the Structure of Political Argument: An Essay and an Annotated Bibliography of Pamphlets on the Allegiance Controversy." *Bulletin of Research in the Humanities* 83, no. 4 (1980): 473–563.

Grant, Ruth. *John Locke's Liberalism.* Chicago: University of Chicago Press, 1987.

———. "Locke's Political Anthropology and Lockean Individualism." *Journal of Politics* 50, no. 1 (1988): 42–63.

Grassi, Ernesto. "The Priority of Common Sense and Imagination: Vico's Philosophical Relevance Today." *Social Research* 43 (1976): 569–70.

———. "Rhetoric and Philosophy." *Philosophy and Rhetoric* 9, no. 4 (1976): 200–216.

———. *Rhetoric as Philosophy.* Translated by John Michael Krois and Azizeh Azodi. Carbondale: Southern Illinois University Press, 1980.

Greenblatt, Stephen. *The Swerve: How the World Became Modern.* New York: Norton, 2011.

Greenfield, Susan C. "Aborting the 'Mother Plot': Politics and Generation in *Absalom and Achitophel.*" *ELH* 62, no. 2 (1995): 267–93.

Habermas, Jürgen. *The Structural Transformation of the Public Sphere: An Inquiry into a Category of Bourgeois Society.* Cambridge: MIT Press, 1989.

Harrison, John, and Peter Laslett, eds. *The Library of John Locke.* Oxford: Clarendon Press, 1971.

Hartle, Ann. *Michel de Montaigne: Accidental Philosopher.* Cambridge: Cambridge University Press, 2003.

Herzog, Don. *Happy Slaves.* Chicago: University of Chicago Press, 1989.

Hirschmann, Nancy. "Intersectionality Before Intersectionality Was Cool: The Importance of Class to Feminist Interpretations of Locke." In *Feminist Interpretations of John Locke,* edited by Nancy Hirschmann and Kirstie McClure, 155–86. University Park: Pennsylvania State University Press, 2007.

Hirschmann, Nancy and Kirstie McClure, editors. *Feminist Interpretations of John Locke.* University Park: Pennsylvania State University Press, 2007.

Hobbes, Thomas. *Leviathan.* Indianapolis: Hackett, 1994.

Howell, Wilbur Samuel. "John Locke and the New Rhetoric." *Quarterly Journal of Speech* 53 (1967): 319–33.

Hsueh, Vicki. "Cultivating and Challenging the Common: Lockean Property, Indigenous Traditionalisms, and the Problem of Exclusion." *Contemporary Political Theory* 5 (2006): 193–214.

———. *Hybrid Constitutions: Challenging Legacies of Law, Privilege, and Culture in Colonial America.* Durham: Duke University Press, 2010.

Huet, Marie-Hélène. *Monstrous Imagination.* Cambridge: Harvard University Press, 1993.

James, Susan. *Passion and Action: The Emotions in Seventeenth-Century Philosophy.* New York: Oxford University Press, 1999.

Johnston, David. *The Rhetoric of "Leviathan": Thomas Hobbes and the Politics of Cultural Transformation.* Princeton: Princeton University Press, 1986.

Jolley, Nicholas. *Locke: His Philosophical Thought.* New York: Oxford University Press, 1999.

Jones, Richard Foster. *The Seventeenth Century: Studies in the History of English Thought and Literature from Bacon to Pope.* Stanford: Stanford University Press, 1951.

Kahn, Victoria Ann. *Wayward Contracts: The Crisis of Political Obligation in England, 1640–1674.* Princeton: Princeton University Press, 2004.

Kant, Immanuel. *Critique of Judgment.* Indianapolis: Hackett, 1987.

Klausen, Jimmy Casas. "Room Enough: America, Natural Liberty, and Consent in Locke's *Second Treatise*." *Journal of Politics* 69, no. 3 (2007): 760–69.

Kroll, Richard W. F. *The Material Word: Literate Culture in the Restoration and Early Eighteenth Century*. Baltimore: Johns Hopkins University Press, 1991.

———. "The Question of Locke's Relation to Gassendi." *Journal of the History of Ideas* 45, no. 3 (1984): 339–59.

Laslett, Peter. Introduction to *Two Treatises of Government*, by John Locke, 3–126. Edited by Peter Laslett. Cambridge: Cambridge University Press, 1988.

Laudan, Laurens. "The Nature and Sources of Locke's Views on Hypotheses." *Journal of the History of Ideas* 28, no. 2 (1967): 211–23.

Law, Jules David. *The Rhetoric of Empiricism: Language and Perception from Locke to I. A. Richards*. Ithaca: Cornell University Press, 1993.

Leites, Edward. *Conscience and Casuistry in Early Modern Europe*. Cambridge: Cambridge University Press, 1988.

Lennon, Thomas M. *The Battle of the Gods and Giants: The Legacies of Descartes and Gassendi, 1655–1715*. Princeton: Princeton University Press, 1993.

Lewis, Rhodri. *Language, Mind, and Nature: Artificial Languages in England from Bacon to Locke*. Cambridge: Cambridge University Press, 2007.

Liebell, Susan. "Lockean Switching: Imagination and the Production of Principles of Toleration." *Perspectives on Politics* 7, no. 4 (2009): 823–36.

Lloyd, Genevieve. *The Man of Reason: "Male" and "Female" in Western Philosophy*. London: Routledge, 1993.

Locke, John. *An Essay Concerning Human Understanding*. Edited by Peter Nidditch. Oxford: Oxford University Press, 1975.

———. "An Examination of Malebranche's Opinion of Seeing All Things in God." In *The Works of John Locke*, new edition, corrected, vol. 9, 211–55. London: Printed for Thomas Tegg, W. Sharpe and Son . . . , 1823.

———. *Locke: Political Essays*. Edited by Mark Goldie. Cambridge: Cambridge University Press, 1997.

———. *Of the Conduct of the Understanding*. Edited by Ruth W. Grant and Nathan Tarcov. Indianapolis: Hackett, 1996.

———. *Some Thoughts Concerning Education*. Edited by Ruth W. Grant and Nathan Tarcov. Indianapolis: Hackett, 1996.

———. *Some Thoughts Concerning Education and Of the Conduct of the Understanding*. Edited by Ruth W. Grant and Nathan Tarcov. Indianapolis: Hackett, 1996.

———. *Two Treatises of Government*. Edited by Peter Laslett. Cambridge: Cambridge University Press, 1988.

Lucretius. *The Way Things Are: The "De Rerum Natura" of Titus Lucretius Carus*. Translated by Rolfe Humphries. Bloomington: Indiana University Press, 1968.

Macpherson, C. B. *The Political Theory of Possessive Individualism: Hobbes to Locke*. Oxford: Oxford University Press, 1962.

Marshall, John. *John Locke: Resistance, Religion, and Responsibility*. Cambridge: Cambridge University Press, 1994.

Martel, James. *Love Is a Sweet Chain: Desire, Autonomy, and Friendship in Liberal Political Theory*. New York: Routledge, 2001.

———. *Subverting Leviathan: Reading Thomas Hobbes as a Radical Democrat*. New York: Columbia University Press, 2007.

Mathiowetz, Dean. *Appeals to Interest: Language, Contestation, and the Shaping of Political Agency*. University Park: Pennsylvania State University Press, 2011.

McClure, Kirstie M. "Cato's Retreat: Fabula, Historia, and the Question of Constitutionalism in Mr Locke's Anonymous *Essay on Government*." In *Reading, Society, and Politics in Early Modern England*, edited by Kevin M. Sharpe and Steven N. Zwicker, 317–50. Cambridge: Cambridge University Press, 2003.

———. *Judging Rights: Lockean Politics and the Limits of Consent*. Ithaca: Cornell University Press, 1996.

Mehta, Uday Singh. *The Anxiety of Freedom: Imagination and Individuality in Locke's Political Thought*. Ithaca: Cornell University Press, 1992.

Mills, Charles. *The Racial Contract*. Ithaca: Cornell University Press, 1997.

Milton, J. R. "Dating Locke's *Second Treatise*." *History of Political Thought* 16, no. 3 (1995): 356–90.

Montaigne, Michel de. "Des cannibales." In *Les essais*, 202–14. Paris: Presses Universitaires de France, 1924.

Nietzsche, Friedrich. "On Truth and Lies in a Extra-moral Sense." In *Friedrich Nietzsche on Rhetoric and Language*, edited and translated by Sander L. Gilman, Carole Blair, and David J. Parent, 246–57. Oxford: Oxford University Press, 1989.

Norval, Aletta. *Aversive Democracy: Inheritance and Originality in the Democratic Tradition*. Cambridge: Cambridge University Press, 2007.

Ott, Walter. *Locke's Philosophy of Language*. Cambridge: Cambridge University Press, 2007.

Panagia, Davide. "The Force of Political Argument." *Political Theory* 32, no. 6 (2004): 825–48.

Pangle, Thomas L. *The Spirit of Modern Republicanism: The Moral Vision of the American Founders and the Philosophy of Locke*. Chicago: University of Chicago Press, 1988.

Pateman, Carole. *The Disorder of Women*. Stanford: Stanford University Press, 1980.

———. *The Sexual Contract*. Stanford: Stanford University Press, 1988.

Pateman, Carole, and Charles Mills. *Contract and Domination*. Cambridge: Polity Press, 2007.

Phiddian, Robert. *Swift's Parody*. Cambridge: Cambridge University Press, 1995.

Pocock, J. G. A. *The Ancient Constitution and the Feudal Law*. Cambridge: Cambridge University Press. 1987.

Rawls, John. *Political Liberalism*. New York: Columbia University Press, 1993.

———. *A Theory of Justice*. Cambridge: Belknap Press of Harvard University Press, 1971.

Regosin, Richard L. *Montaigne's Unruly Brood: Textual Engendering and the Challenge to Paternal Authority*. Berkeley and Los Angeles: University of California Press, 1996.

Remer, Gary. *Humanism and the Rhetoric of Toleration*. University Park: Pennsylvania State University Press, 1996.

Ricchetti, John. *Philosophical Writing: Locke, Berkeley, Hume*. Cambridge: Harvard University Press, 1983.

Rogin, Michael. "Liberal Society and the Indian Question." In *Ronald Reagan: The Movie and Other Episodes in Political Demonology*, 134–68. Berkeley and Los Angeles: University of California Press, 1987.

Rorty, Richard. *Philosophy and the Mirror of Nature*. Princeton: Princeton University Press, 1979.

Rose, Margaret A. *Parody: Ancient, Modern, and Post-modern*. Cambridge: Cambridge University Press, 1993.

Ross, Ian Campbell. "'A Very Knowing American': The Inca Garcilaso de la Vega and Swift's *Modest Proposal*." *Modern Language Quarterly* 68, no. 4 (2007): 493–516.

Sarasohn, Lisa T. "Motion and Morality: Pierre Gassendi, Thomas Hobbes, and the Mechanical World-View." *Journal of the History of Ideas* 46, no. 3 (1985): 363–79.

Schochet, Gordon. *Patriarchalism in Political Thought: The Authoritarian Family and Political Speculation and Attitudes Especially in Seventeenth-Century England*. Oxford: Blackwell, 1975.

Scott, Jonathan. *Commonwealth Principles: Republican Writing of the English Revolution*. Cambridge: Cambridge University Press, 2004.

———. "The Law of War: Grotius, Sidney, Locke, and the Political Theory of Rebellion." *History of Political Thought* 13 (1992): 565–85.

Seliger, Martin. *The Liberal Politics of John Locke*. New York: Frederick A. Praeger, 1968.

Sellars, Wilfred. *Empiricism and the Philosophy of Mind*. Cambridge: Harvard University Press, 1997.

Serjeantson, R. W. "Testimony and Proof in Early-Modern England." *Studies in History and Philosophy of Science* 30, no. 2 (1999): 195–36.

Seth, Vanita. *Europe's Indians: Producing Racial Difference, 1500–1900*. Durham: Duke University Press, 2010.

Shanks, Torrey. "Consent." In *Encyclopedia of Political Thought*, edited by Michael T. Gibbons. Oxford: Wiley Blackwell, forthcoming, 2014.

————. "Feminine Figures and the 'Fatherhood': Rhetoric and Reason in Locke's *First Treatise of Government.*" *Political Theory* 39, no. 1 (2011): 31–57.

————. "Toleration and Democratic Membership: Locke and Montaigne on Judging Monsters." *Political Theory*, forthcoming.

Shapin, Steven. *The Scientific Revolution.* Chicago: University of Chicago Press, 1996.

Shapin, Steven and Simon Schaffer. *Leviathan and the Air-Pump.* Princeton: Princeton University Press, 1985.

Shapiro, Barbara. *A Culture of Fact: England, 1550–1720.* Ithaca: Cornell University Press, 2003.

————. *Probability and Certainty in Seventeenth-Century England.* Princeton: Princeton University Press, 1985.

Shuger, Debora K. *Sacred Rhetoric: The Christian Grand Style in the English Renaissance.* Princeton: Princeton University Press, 1988.

Sidney, Philip. *Defense of Poetry.* In *The Works of Sir Philip Sidney,* edited by A. Feuillerat, vol. 3. Cambridge: Cambridge University Press, 1912–26.

Skinner, Daniel. "Political Theory Beyond the Reason-Rhetoric Divide: Hobbes, Semantic Indeterminacy, and Political Order." *Review of Politics* 73, no. 4 (2011): 561–80.

Skinner, Quentin. *The Foundations of Modern Political Thought.* Vol. 1. Cambridge: Cambridge University Press, 1978.

————. *Reason and Rhetoric in the Philosophy of Hobbes.* New York: Cambridge University Press, 1996.

Sprat, Thomas. *History of the Royal Society.* Edited by Jackson I. Cope and Harold Whitmore Jones. St. Louis: Washington University Press, 1958.

Stanton, Timothy. "Authority and Freedom in the Interpretation of Locke's Political Theory." *Political Theory* 39, no. 1 (2011): 6–30.

Strauss, Leo. *Natural Right and History.* Chicago: University of Chicago Press, 1953.

Tarcov, Nathan. *Locke's Education for Liberty.* Chicago: University of Chicago Press, 1987.

Tarlton, Charles D. "A Rope of Sand: Interpreting Locke's *First Treatise of Government.*" *Historical Journal* 21, no. 1 (1978): 43–73.

Taylor, Charles. *Sources of the Self: The Making of the Modern Identity.* Cambridge: Harvard University Press, 1992.

Thompson, Helen. "'In Idea, a Thousand Nameless Joys': Secondary Qualities in Arnauld, Locke, and Haywood's *Lasselia.*" *Eighteenth Century* 48, no. 3 (2007): 225–43.

Tuck, Richard. "A New Date for Filmer's *Patriarcha.*" *Historical Journal* 29, no. 1 (1986): 183–86.

Tully, James. *An Approach to Political Philosophy: Locke in Contexts.* Cambridge: Cambridge University Press, 1993.

————. *A Discourse on Property.* Cambridge: Cambridge University Press, 1980.

————. "Governing Conduct." In *An Approach to Political Philosophy: Locke in Contexts,* 179–241. Cambridge: Cambridge University Press, 1993.

————. *Public Philosophy in a New Key.* 2 vols. Cambridge: Cambridge University Press, 2008.

————. *Strange Multiplicity: Constitutionalism in an Age of Diversity.* Cambridge: Cambridge University Press, 1995.

Tuveson, Ernest. *Imagination as a Means of Grace: Locke and the Aesthetics of Romanticism.* New York: Gordian Press, 1974.

————. "Locke and Sterne." In *Reason and the Imagination: Studies in the History of Ideas, 1600–1800,* edited by J. A. Mazzeo, 255–77. New York: Columbia University Press, 1962.

————. "Locke and the Dissolution of the Ego." *Modern Philology* 52, no. 3 (1955): 159–74.

Vickers, Brian. "The Royal Society and English Prose Style: A Reassessment." In *Rhetoric and the Pursuit of Truth: Language Change in the Seventeenth and Eighteenth Centuries,* edited by Brian Vickers and Nancy Struever, 3–76. Los Angeles: Clark Memorial Library, 1985.

Vogt, Philip. *John Locke and the Rhetoric of Modernity.* Lanham, Md.: Lexington Books, 2008.

Waldron, Jeremy. *God, Locke, and Equality.* Cambridge: Cambridge University Press, 2003.

————. "John Locke: Social Contract Versus Political Anthropology." In *The Social Contract from Hobbes to Rawls,* edited by David Boucher and Paul Kelly, 51–72. London: Routledge, 1994.

Walker, William. *Locke, Literary Criticism, and Philosophy.* Cambridge: Cambridge University Press, 1994.

Walmsley, Peter. "Locke's Cassowary and the *Ethos* of the *Essay*." *Studies in Eighteenth Century Culture* 22 (1993): 253–67.

———. *Locke's "Essay" and the Rhetoric of Science*. Lewisburg: Bucknell University Press, 2003.

Weiskel, Thomas. *The Romantic Sublime: Studies in the Structure and Psychology of Transcendence*. Baltimore: Johns Hopkins University Press, 1976.

Wingrove, Elizabeth. *Rousseau's Republican Romance*. Princeton: Princeton University Press, 2000.

Wolterstorff, Nicholas. *John Locke and the Ethics of Belief*. New York: Cambridge University Press, 1996.

Wood, Neal. *The Politics of Locke's Philosophy: A Social Study of "An Essay Concerning Human Understanding."* Berkeley and Los Angeles: University of California Press, 1983.

Wootton, David. Introduction to *John Locke: Political Writings*, by John Locke, 5–122. Indianapolis: Hackett, 2003.

Wright, Joanne H. "Recovering Locke's Midwifery Notes." In *Feminist Interpretations of John Locke*, edited by Nancy Hirschmann and Kirstie McClure, 213–40. University Park: Pennsylvania State University Press, 2007.

Yolton, John. *John Locke and the Way of Ideas*. Oxford: Clarendon Press, 1956.

———. *Locke and the Compass of Human Understanding: A Selective Commentary on the "Essay."* Cambridge: Cambridge University Press, 1970.

———. *Perception and Reality: A History from Descartes to Kant*. Ithaca: Cornell University Press, 1996.

———. *Thinking Matter: Materialism in Eighteenth-Century Britain*. Minneapolis: University of Minnesota Press, 1983.

Zerilli, Linda. *Feminism and the Abyss of Freedom*. Chicago: University of Chicago Press, 2005.

———. "'Philosophy's Gaudy Dress.'" *European Journal of Political Theory* 4, no. 2 (2005): 146–63.

———. "Response to Reply by Terrell Carver." *European Journal of Political Theory* 5, no. 4 (2006): 479–82.

———. *Signifying Woman: Culture and Chaos in Rousseau, Burke, and Mill*. Ithaca: Cornell University Press, 1994.

Zuckert, Michael. "An Introduction to Locke's *First Treatise*." In *John Locke: Critical Assessments*, vol. 3, edited by Richard Ashcraft, 121–37. London: Routledge, 1991.

———. *Launching Liberalism: On Lockean Political Philosophy*. Lawrence: University Press of Kansas, 2002.

Zwicker, Steven. *Lines of Authority: Politics and English Literary Culture, 1649–1689*. Ithaca: Cornell University Press, 1993.

INDEX